flaminio gundy

Asolo hills
Where the art challenges the seasons

Asolo hills
Where the art challenges the seasons

by Flaminio Gundy

All rights reserved.
No part of this book may be used or reproduced in any manner without written permission of the publisher.

Copyright © 2019 by Flaminio Gundy

Kindle Direct Publishing, USA, 2019

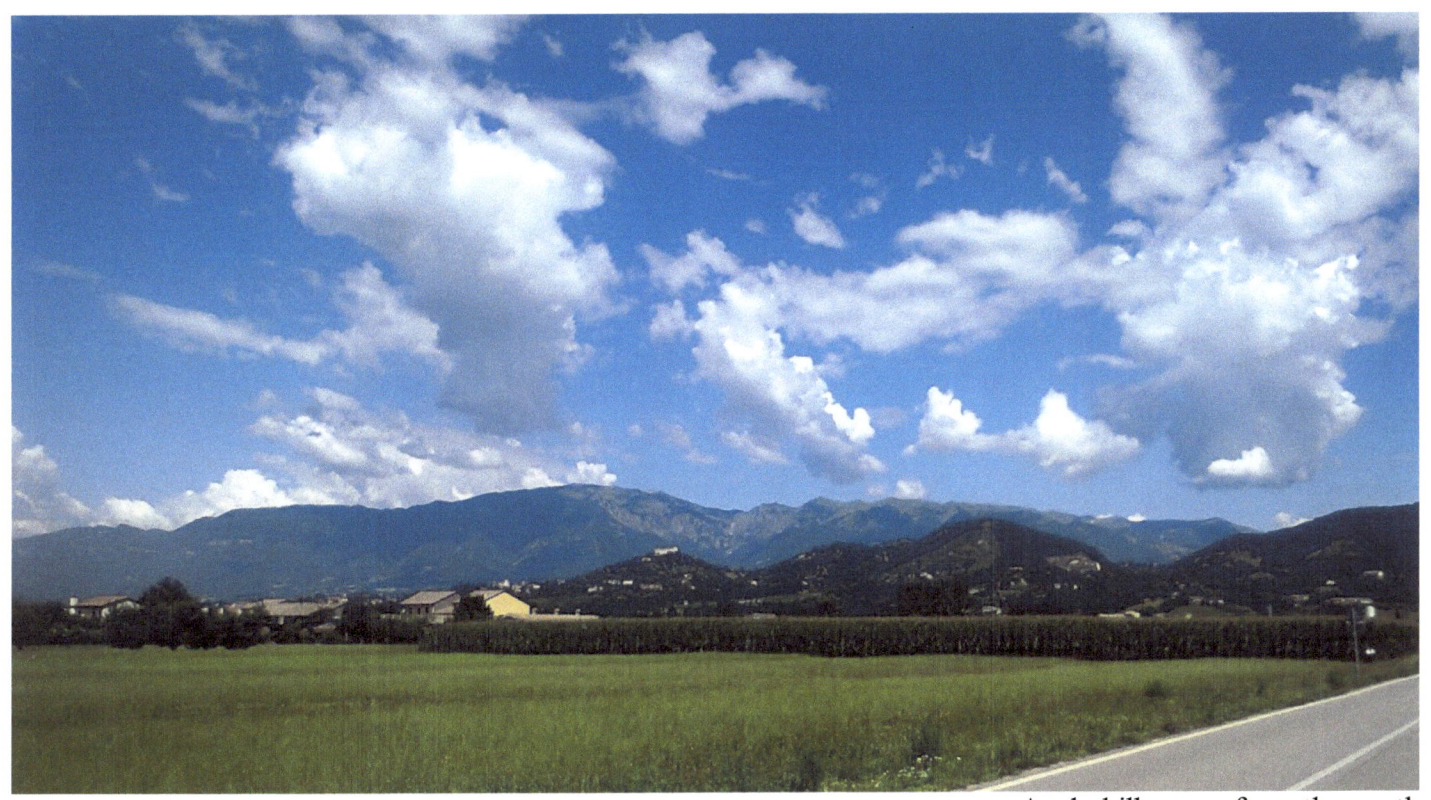
Asolo hills, seen from the south

Baccalà mantecato, creamed cod. It is prepared with stockfish, an arctic cod of Norwegian origin that is preserved by drying with cold air. The name stoccafisso derives from the Norwegian stokkfisk, a stick fish, but in the Veneto the stockfish is commonly called baccalà, hence the name of the recipe. Stockfish, which is often sold whole, requires a prolonged soaking in cold, running water before it can be cooked and consumed.
To prepare the Venetian cod, soak the stockfish for at least 24 hours in soaking in running water or changing the soak frequently. Then cut it into pieces and place in a pan covering it with cold water and a little milk to taste, salt lightly and bring to a boil, skimming from time to time. Cook the cod for about 30 minutes, until it is well cooked and tender. Drain the cod and clean it, depriving it of the bones and the skin, then reduce into small pieces and place in a bowl. With a wooden spoon (or in a planetary mixer) vigorously mix the cod, adding oil at flush, as in the preparation of a mayonnaise. You will get a compact and homogeneous cream with a shiny appearance and a few whole pieces. Season with salt and pepper and add chopped parsley and garlic.

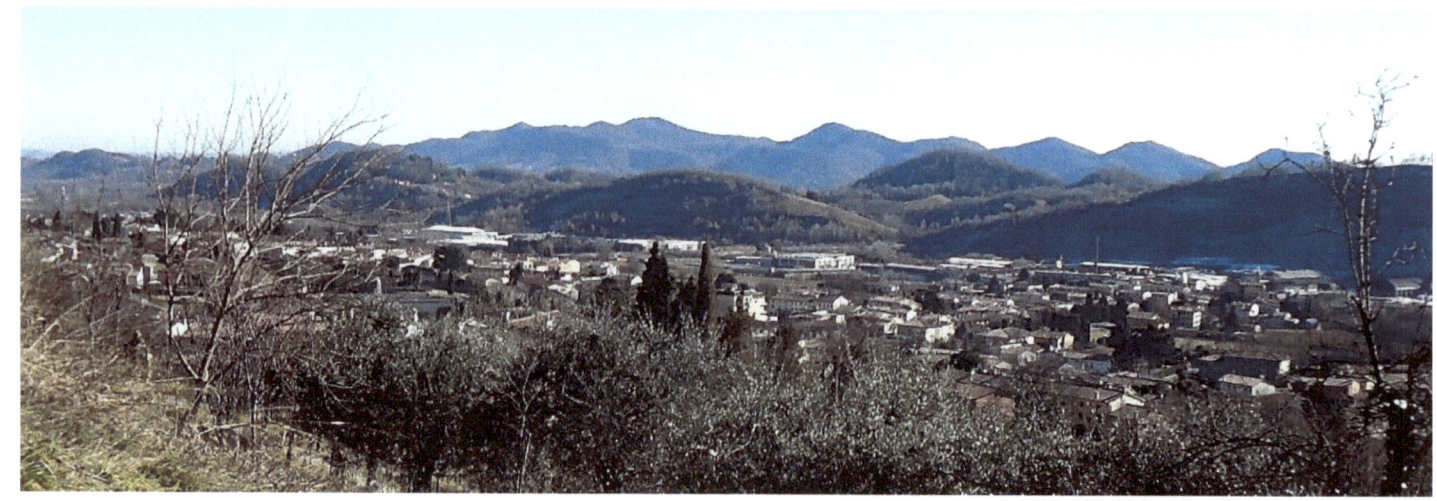

Asolo hills, seen from the north

Ovi e sparasi, eggs and asparagus. Carefully wash and peel the asparagus, remove them from the harder, woody part of the stem so that, once cooked, only the softest part is left without any filament. Make 4 small bunches, tie them with kitchen string and place vertically in a tall, narrow pot, in salted and boiling water, with the tips pointing upwards, but out of water, because heat and steam are sufficient to cook them. Let them boil for about 15 minutes, then remove them from the water and wrap in a cloth to complete their cooking and at the same time deprive of excess water. Separately boil the eggs for 8 minutes, remove them from the heat, cool them under a jet of cold water so that the yolk remains soft and then shell them. Put a small bunch of asparagus on each plate without the string and two eggs. Each diner will then crush the eggs with a fork to obtain a rather homogeneous cream that he will season with a little olive oil, salt, pepper and a drop of vinegar.

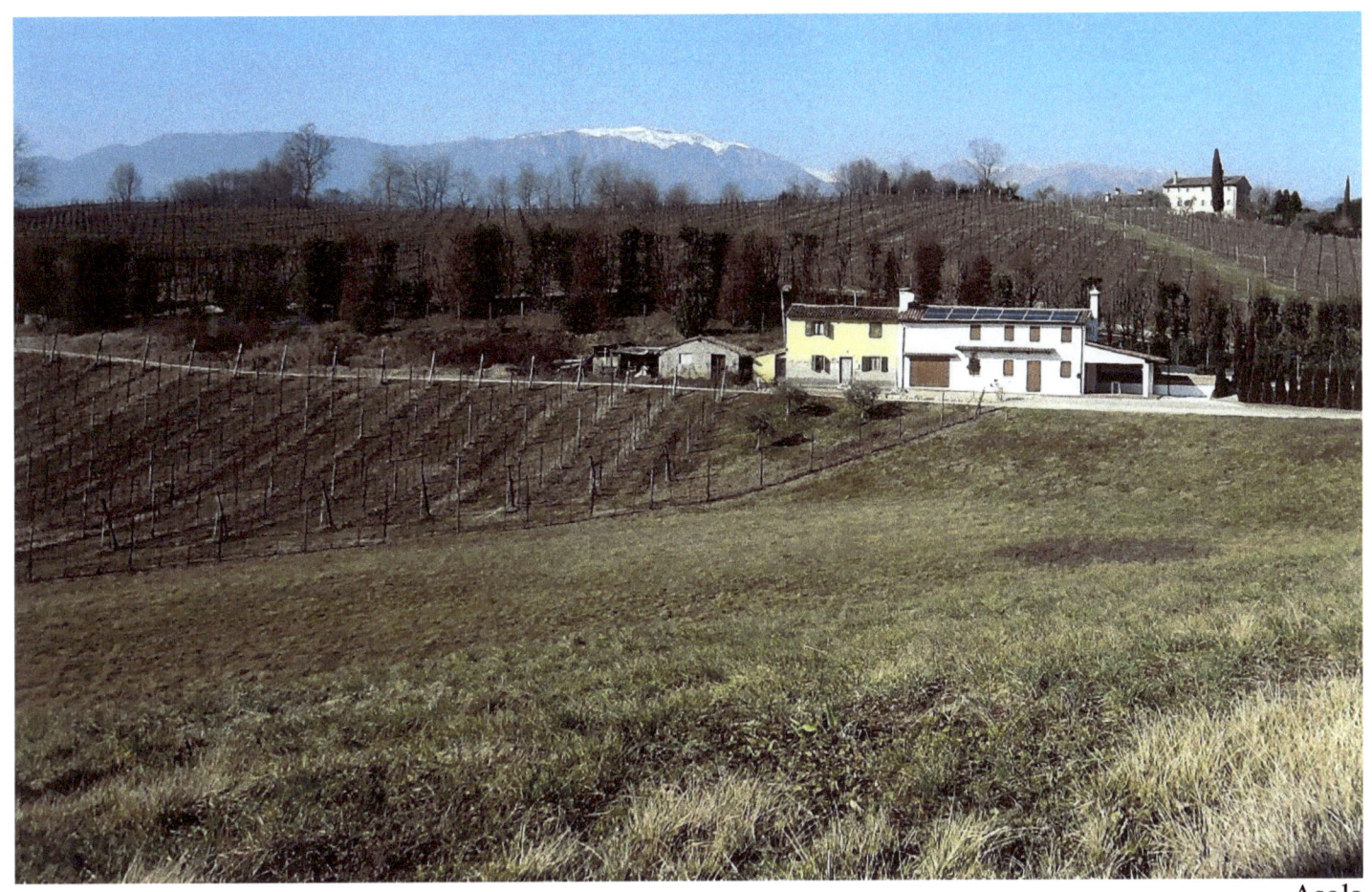
Asolo

Sopressa coa poenta, sopressa with polenta. In the cold months the polenta goes very well with the sopressa. Bring 1.2 liters of salted water to a boil in a saucepan, pour 300 gr. of corn flour and cook the polenta for a little less than an hour, stirring with the appropriate stick or with a wooden spoon. When the polenta is ready pour it on a cutting board and let it cool for an hour. Melt the butter in a pan and when it is bubbly put the slices of sopressa to brown, turning them over, then moisten them with the vinegar letting it evaporate over medium heat. Cut 8 slices out of polenta, place them on a red-hot grill and grill them, turning with a spatula. Distribute them on the plates together with the sopressa and its dressing and serve.

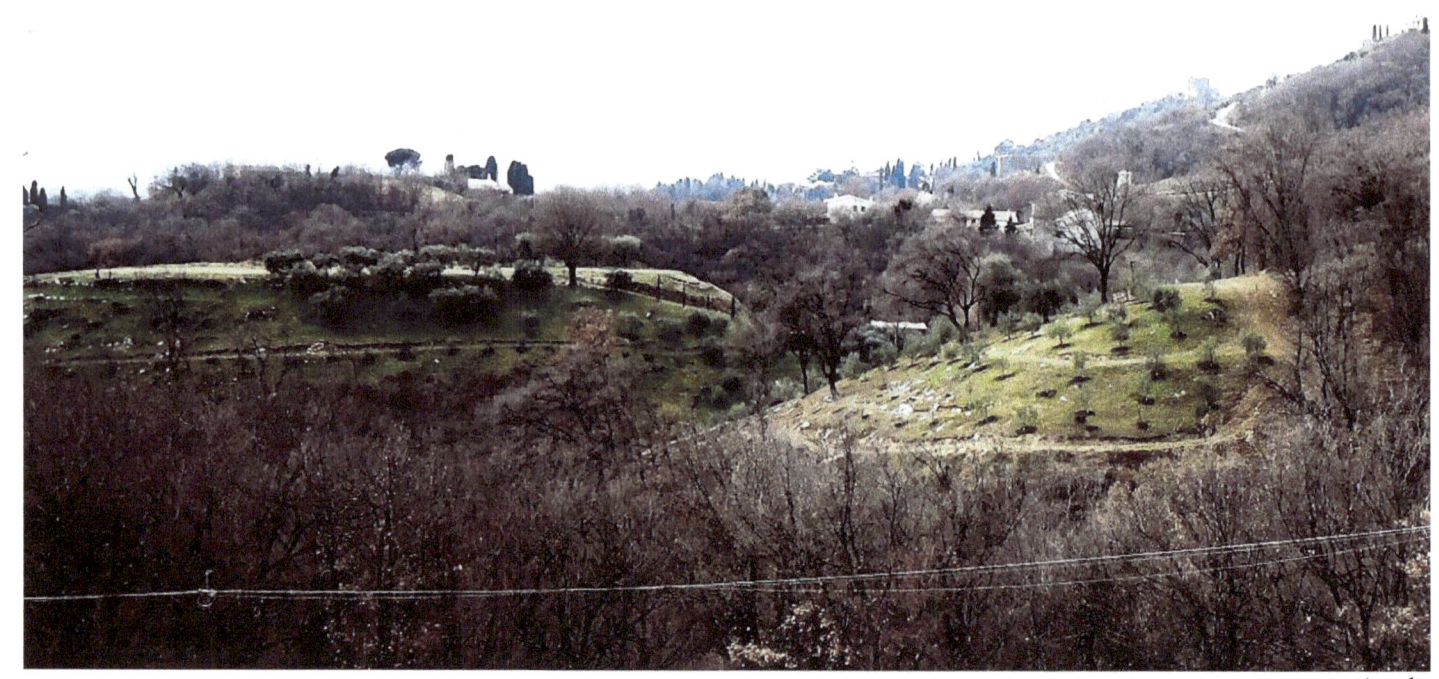
Asolo

Bigoi co l'arna, spaghetti with duck. Bigoli are a typical Venetian long pasta that reminds of spaghettoni with a rough and rather porous surface that absorbs the seasoning well. The traditional bigoli are packaged by hand using a special press called the *bigolaro*. They are prepared with eggs, flour, butter, water and salt. They should not be cooked in boiling water but in the fat broth of the duck and finally seasoned with flavored butter and duck offal. Brown the onion with oil and add the ground duck, white wine, salt, pepper, sage, rosemary and cook for an hour. Boil the salted water in a separate saucepan, add the bigoli and drain al dente. Finally, sauté everything for a few minutes and serve.

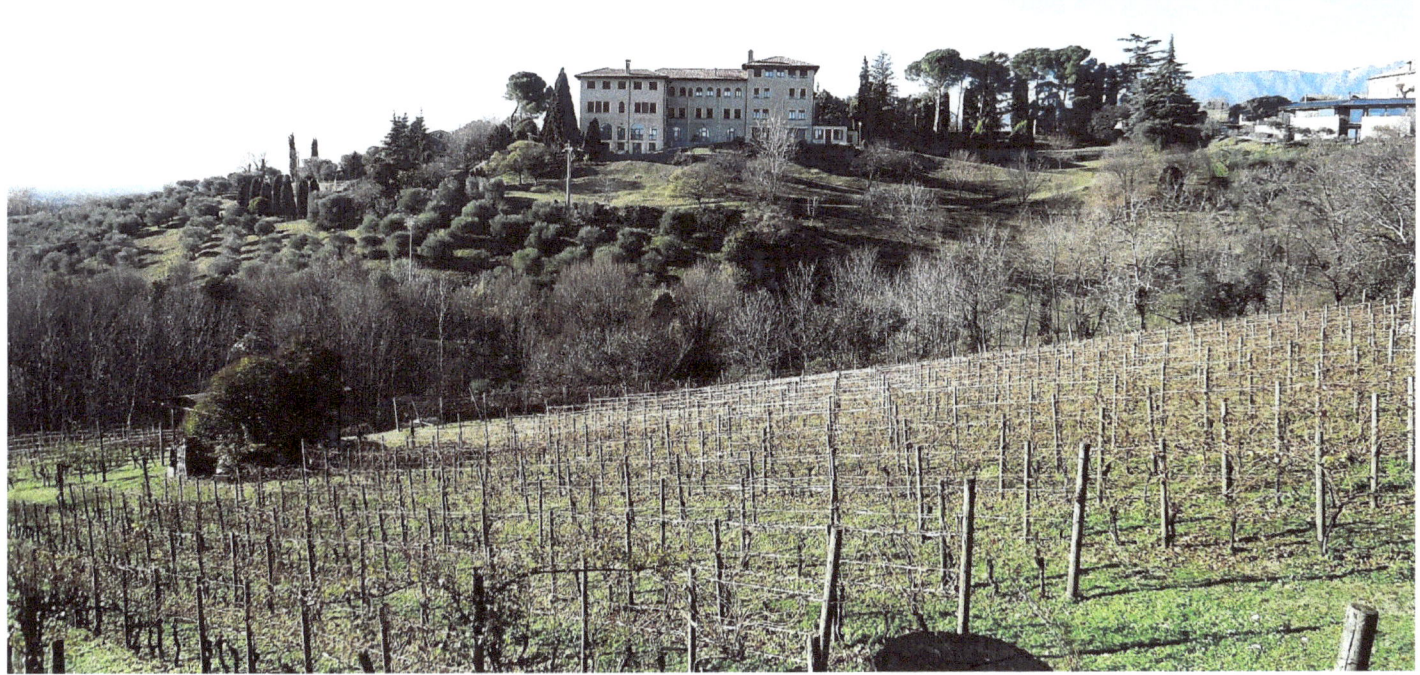

Asolo

Bìgoi in salsa, spaghetti in sauce. Drain the anchovies, remove the bones and the scales. Peel the white onion and slice it thinly. Pour the olive oil in a non-stick pan and add the onion, browning it slightly, then add the anchovies and brown them. Sprinkle with white wine, cover the saucepan, reduce the heat and cook slowly, stirring often until the sauce is creamy, homogeneous and well blended. In the meantime boil the bigoli in plenty of lightly salted water and drain them al dente. Transfer them to the pan with the hot anchovy sauce and mix well so that the bigoli are seasoned by absorbing the sauce. To make the dish even tastier, you can add breadcrumbs sautéed in olive oil or chopped parsley or a sprinkling of black pepper.

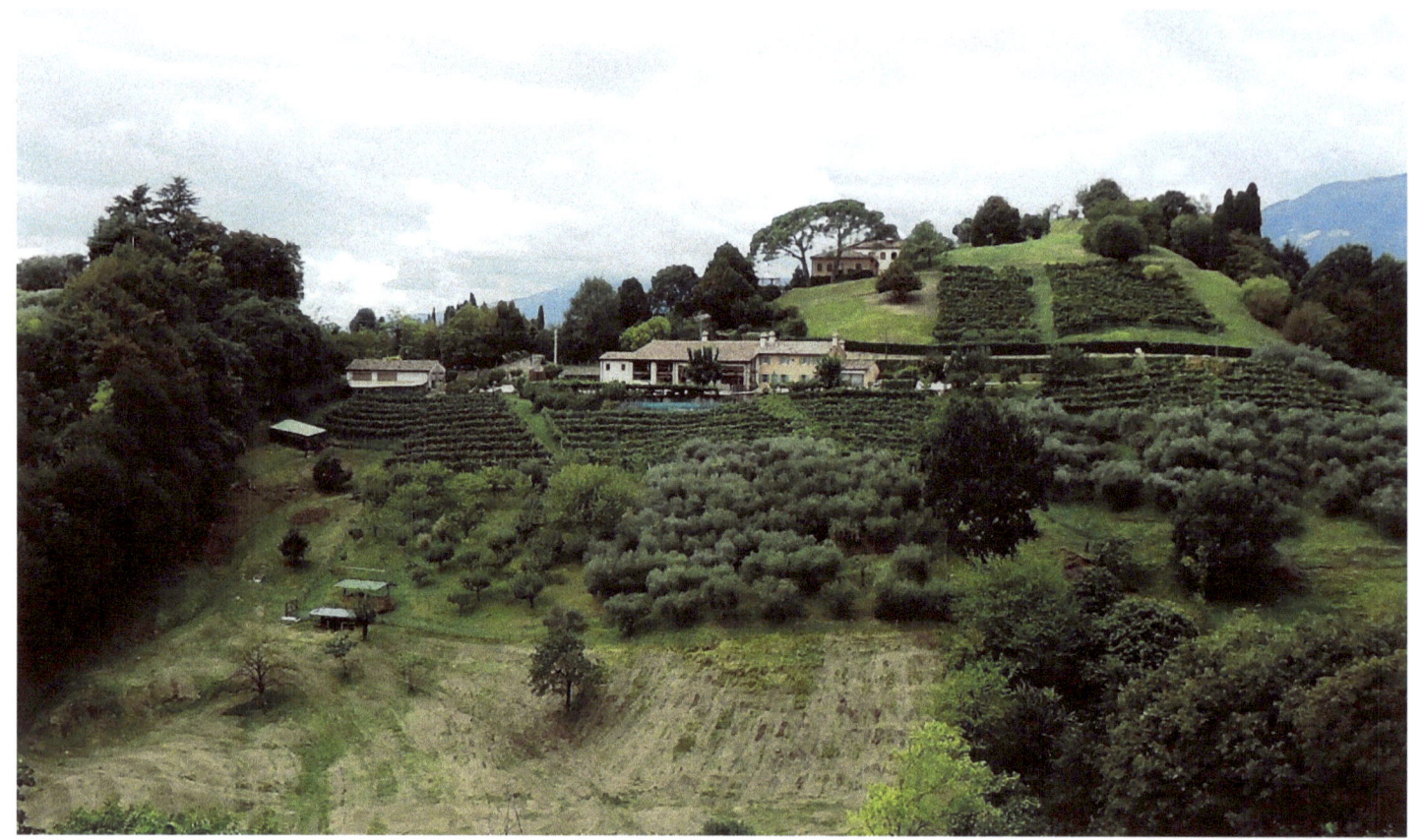
Asolo

Gnochi de patate, potato gnocchi. Wash the potatoes and boil them in a saucepan. Peel and pass them through a vegetable mill. Let the dough cool, then mix it well with the flour and parmesan until it is compact and soft. Make long, one-inch rolls, align them next to each other and cut them into rectangular cubes with a floured knife. On the reverse side of a cheese grater, squeeze each dumpling with a light push of the thumb, thus forming the classic striped gnocchi on the outside. Let them rest for a few minutes, then pour them into boiling salted water and collect them when they emerge on the surface with a sieve. Place them in layers in a baking dish and sprinkle them with grated cheese and boiling melted butter.

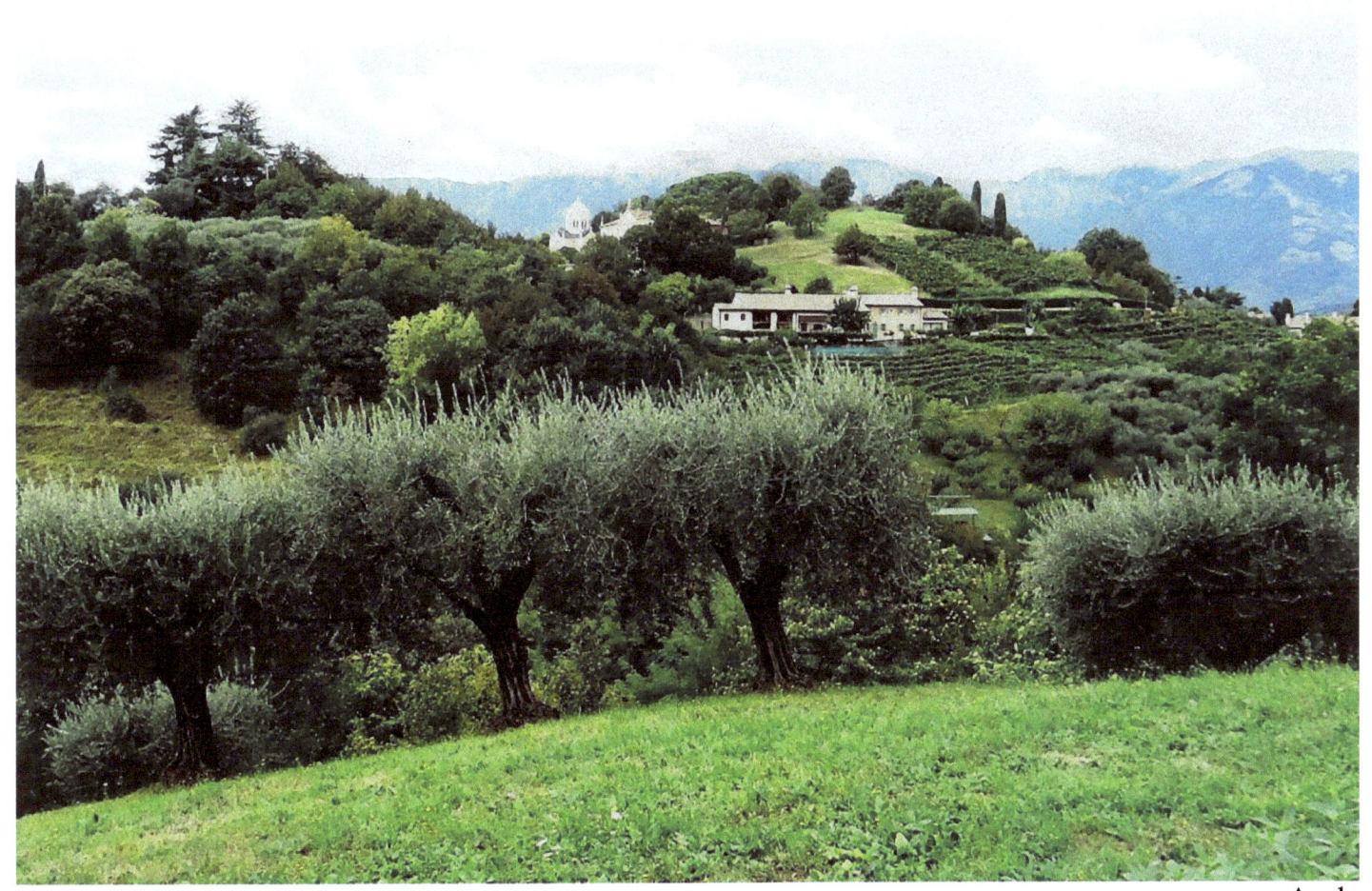

Asolo

Minestra di zucca, pumpkin soup. First you will have to prepare the pumpkin, peeling it and cutting it into pieces. Then boil it in a saucepan with a little water until it becomes soft. Drain and pass it to the mixer to reduce it to a pulp. Boil the milk In a saucepan and add the pumpkin mush, stirring well over medium heat. When the boiling occurs again, lower the heat and cook the pasta in the same pot. Salt and when cooking the pasta add the butter stirring well. Then serve in a dish still warm with some grated Parmesan and some black pepper.

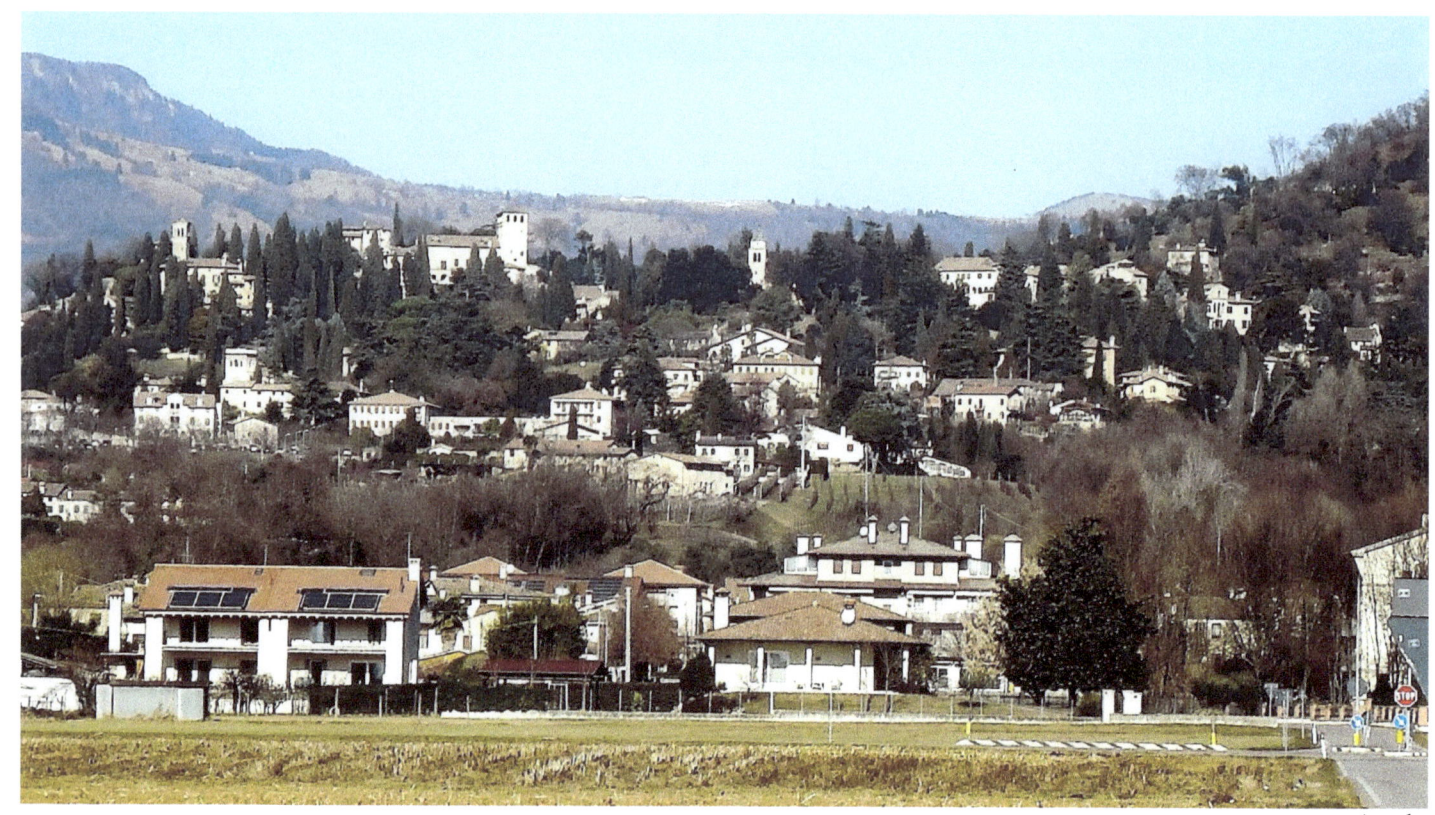
Asolo

Panada. Cut the bread into small pieces and let it cook on a low heat for about an hour in the meat broth, then season with butter and grated cheese. You can also prepare panada with chicken broth, vegetable broth or simply boiling water. If you want to make the dish even more inviting, you can add fresh or frozen peas to the boiling liquid. Add the butter and cheese to taste, mix well and serve immediately.

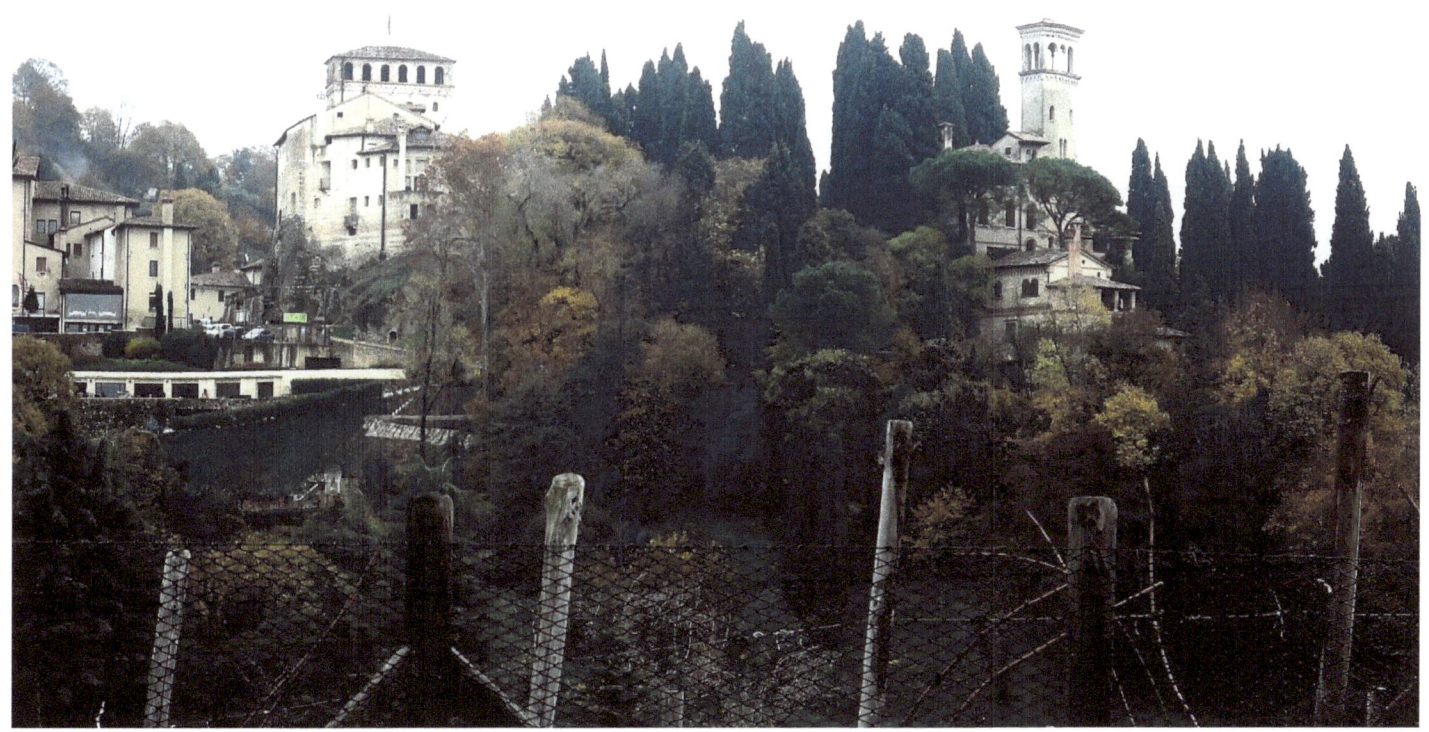

Asolo

Pasta e fasoi, pasta and beans. Soak the dried borlotti beans in plenty of cold water and let them rest overnight. Then put the beans back in a saucepan, cover them with water, add the onion, the carrot and the chopped celery, the lard and salt. Place on the heat and bring to a boil, removing the foam that forms on the surface. When cooked, the broth should be thick and to make it as you can, at the end, sift a part of the beans through and put them back in the pot. At this point, put the tagliatelle in the saucepan and cook for a few minutes. When the preparation is ready, place the *pasta e fasoi* in the dishes of diners, distributing to each a piece of lard, a spoonful of raw oil and a little pepper.

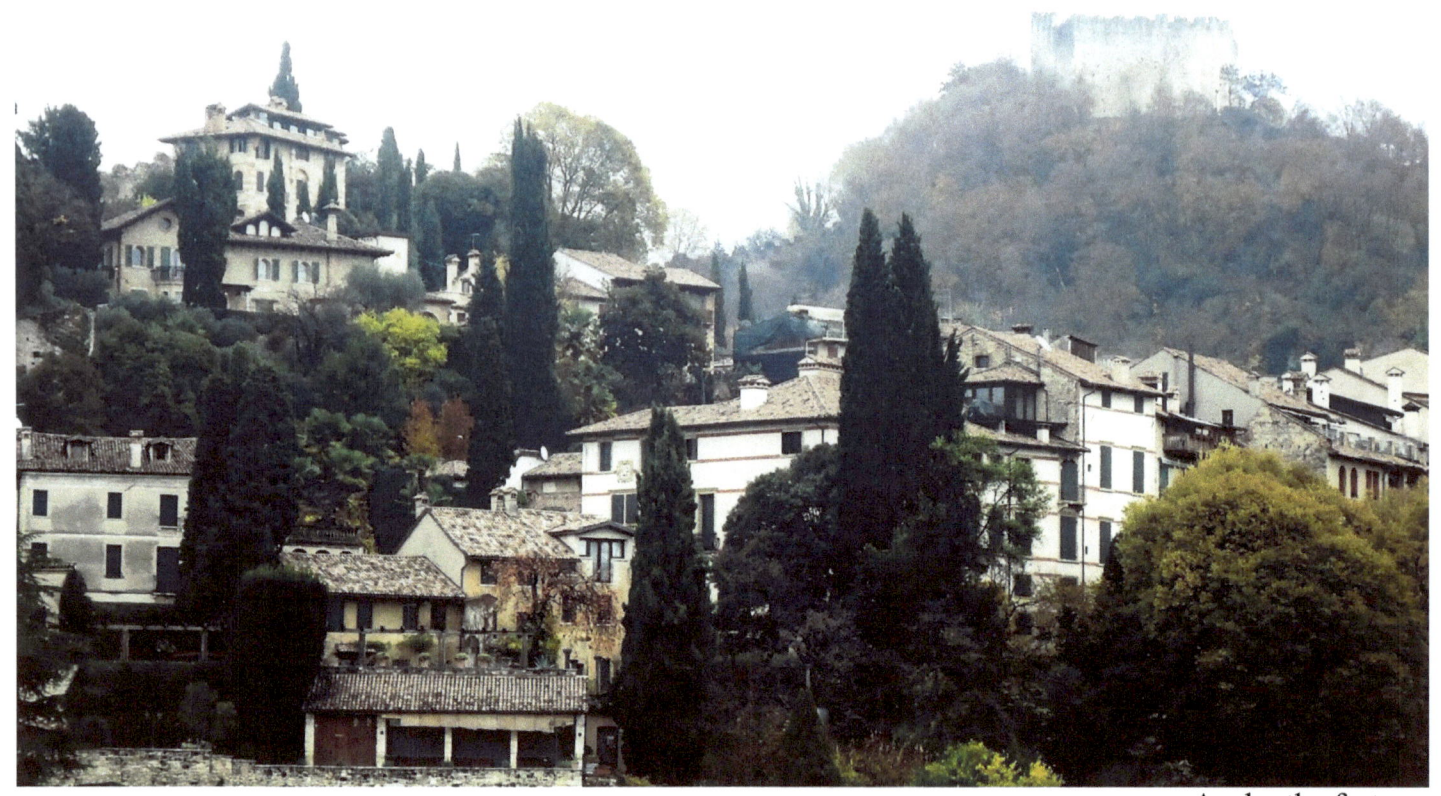

Asolo, the fortress

Risi e bisi, rice and peas. Peel the onion and cut it finely, then wash the parsley, dry it and chop it with the help of a half-moon. Finally cut the bacon (or lard) into cubes. Put in a saucepan 20 grams of butter, the oil, the chopped bacon, the onion and the parsley. Brown all together, stirring and paying attention that it does not burn. Once the mixture is ready, add the peas and cook over low heat for about ten minutes, then pour the broth and bring to a boil. Add the rice, stirring constantly so as not to stick it, and gradually add more boiling broth, if necessary, until the rice is cooked. Once cooked, season with salt and stir in the remaining butter and grated cheese. Let stand a few minutes then serve on the table.

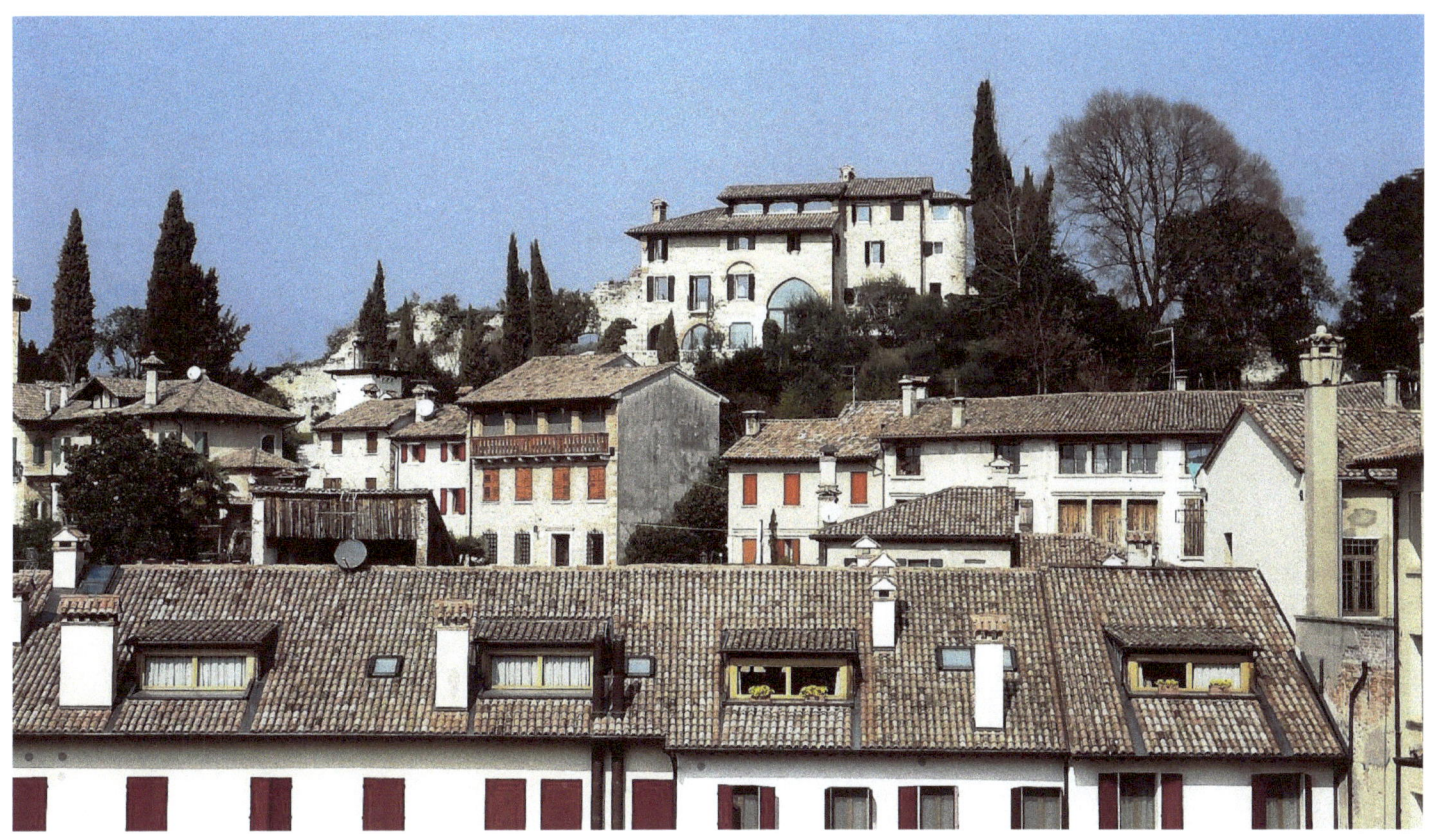
Asolo

Risi, verze e luganega, rice, Savoy cabbage and sausage. Boil the broth, cut the cabbage into strips and then into squares, peel the shallot and chop it coarsely. Cook the shallots and cabbage in a pan for about 4 minutes with a dash of broth, salt and pepper. Toast the rice in a pan with oil and salt, add the white wine and then the broth a little at a time to cook it. Halfway through cooking, add the cabbage. In the meantime, pierce the sausages with a fork, brown them in a pan to let out some of the fat, peel and break them into small pieces. When cooked, stir in the rice with butter and cheese, keeping it rather watery, add the crumbled sausage and decorate with freshly ground pepper and raw Savoy cabbage cut into strips.

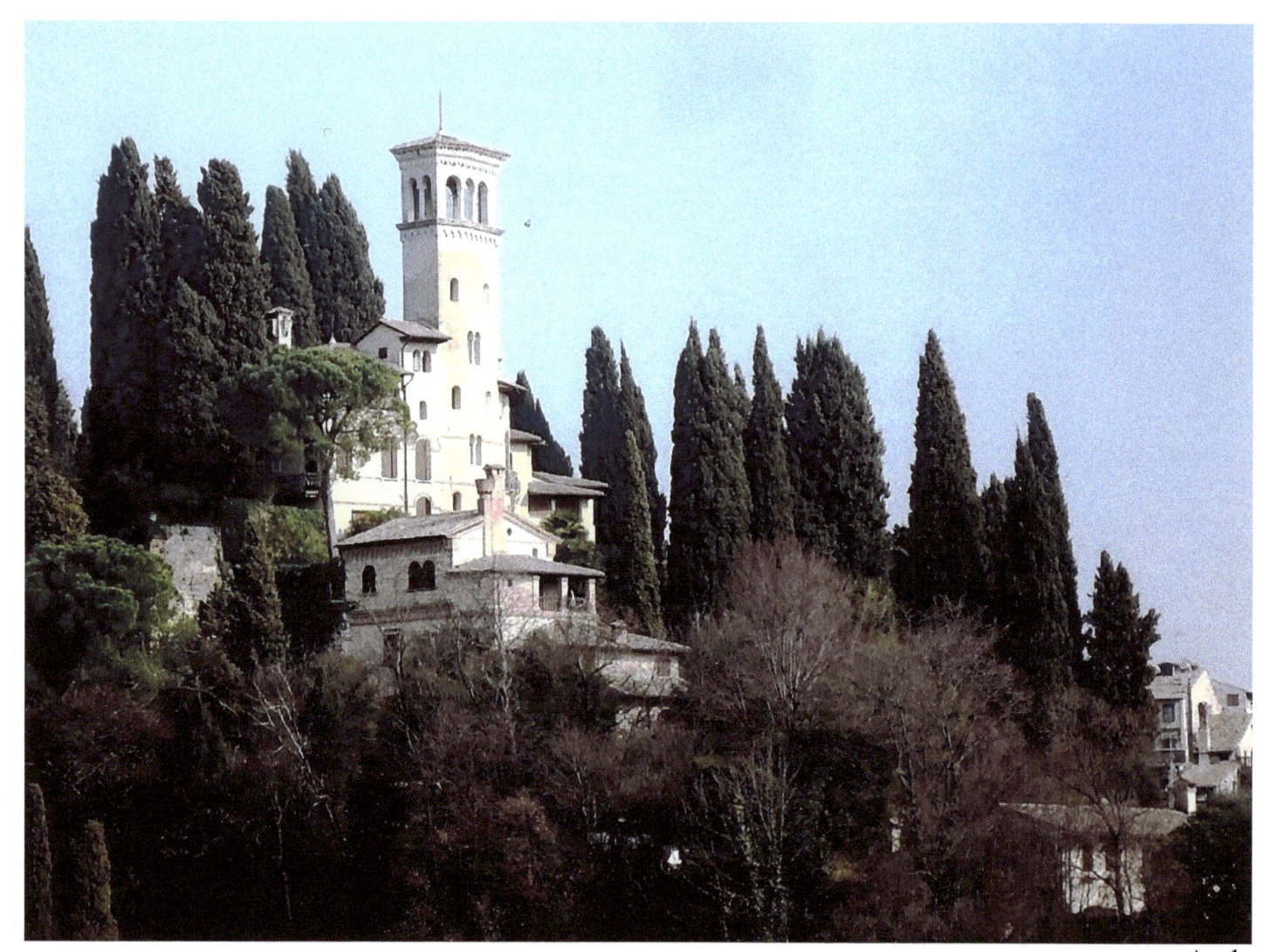
Asolo

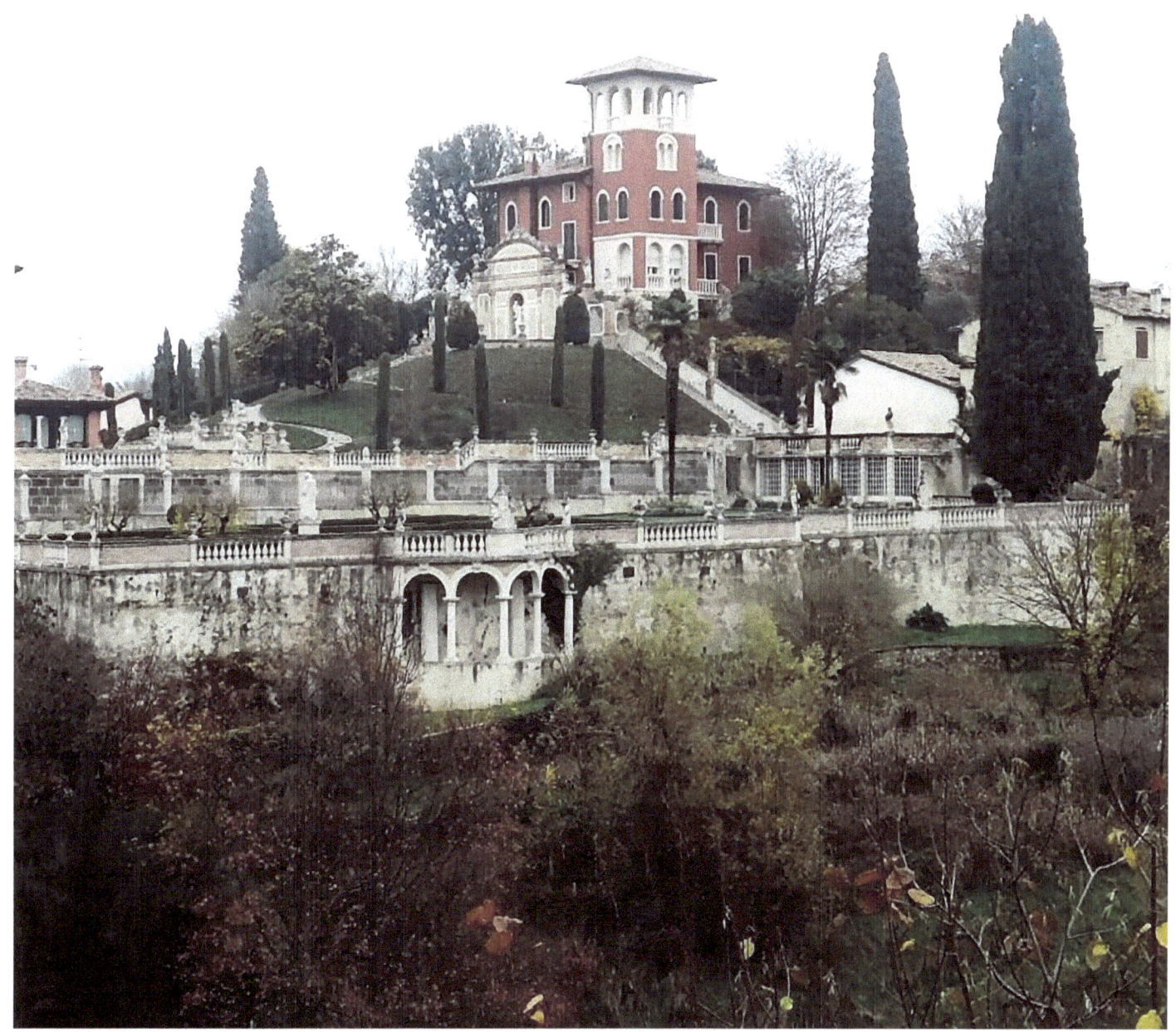

Asolo

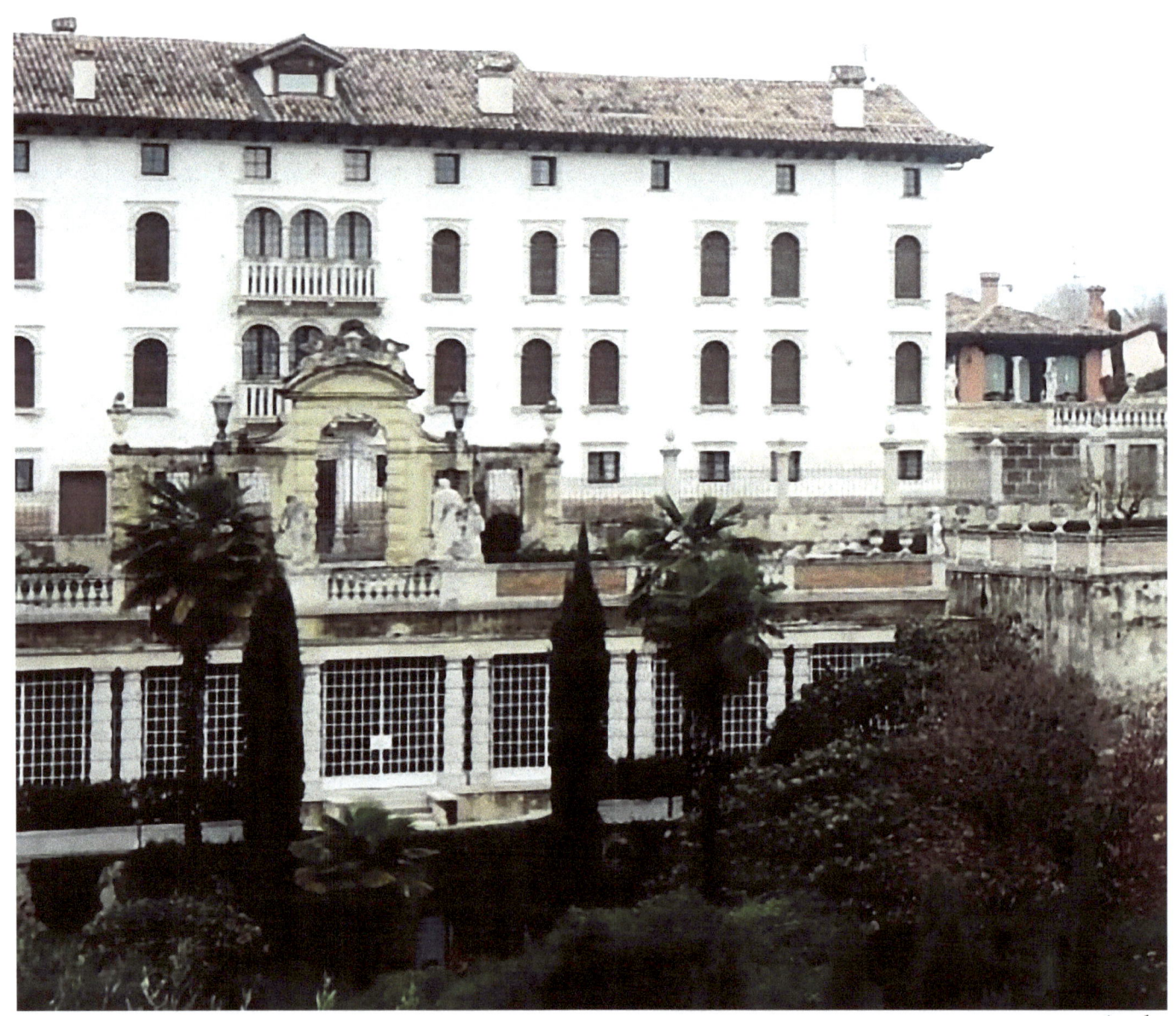
Asolo

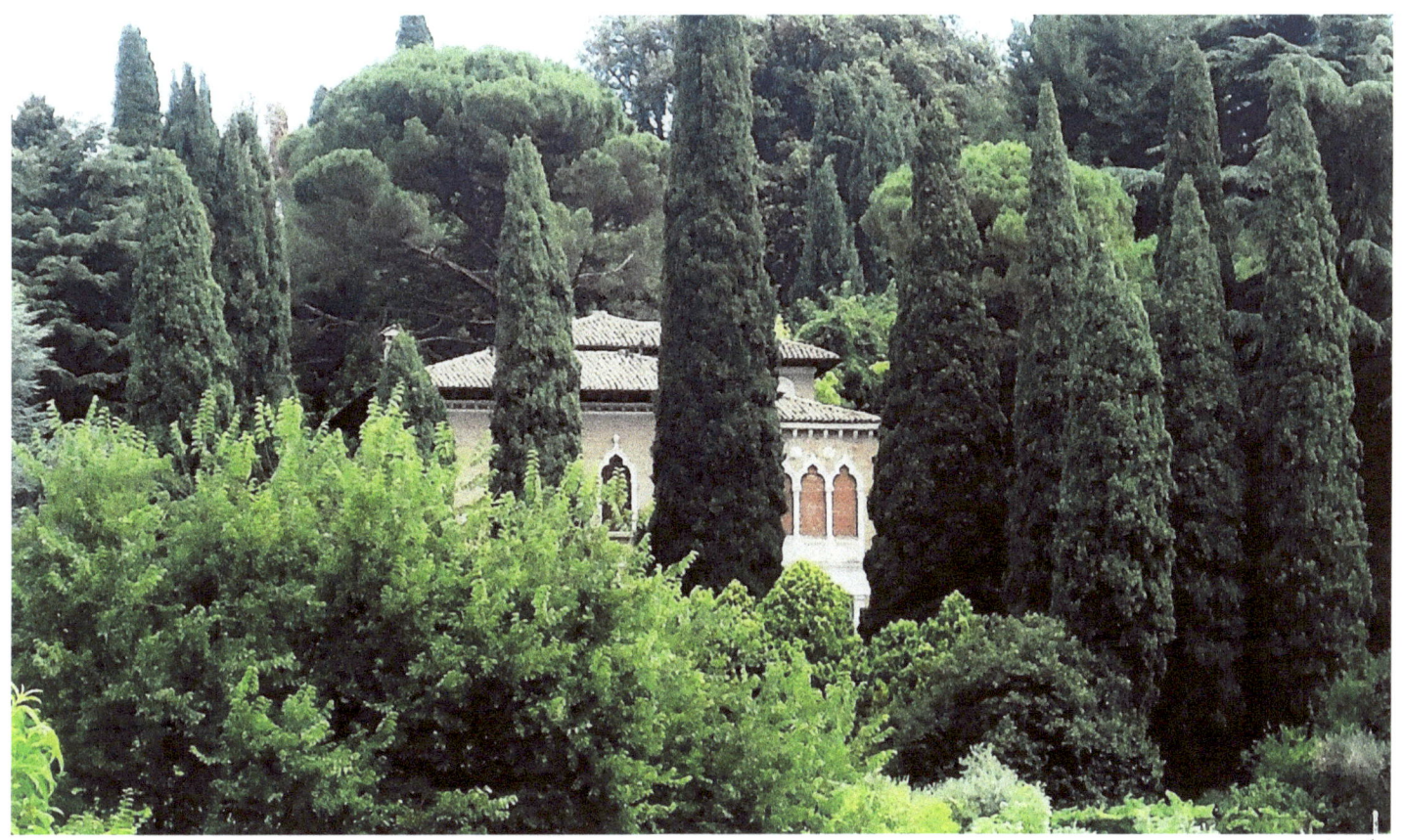
Asolo

Risoto coi bruscandoi, risotto with hop sprouts. Fry the chopped parsley in the oil, then pour in the garlic and the well washed and chopped hop tips. Cook at a moderate heat for at least a quarter of an hour. Pour the rice and stir, raise the heat to toast it then add the broth little by little (never more than half a ladle for each addition) and wait until the rice has incorporated it all before adding more. Always keep stirring and just before the rice is cooked, adjust the salting, pour in the grated parmesan, pepper and butter. At this point, turn off the heat, cover with the lid and let stand for two minutes before serving.

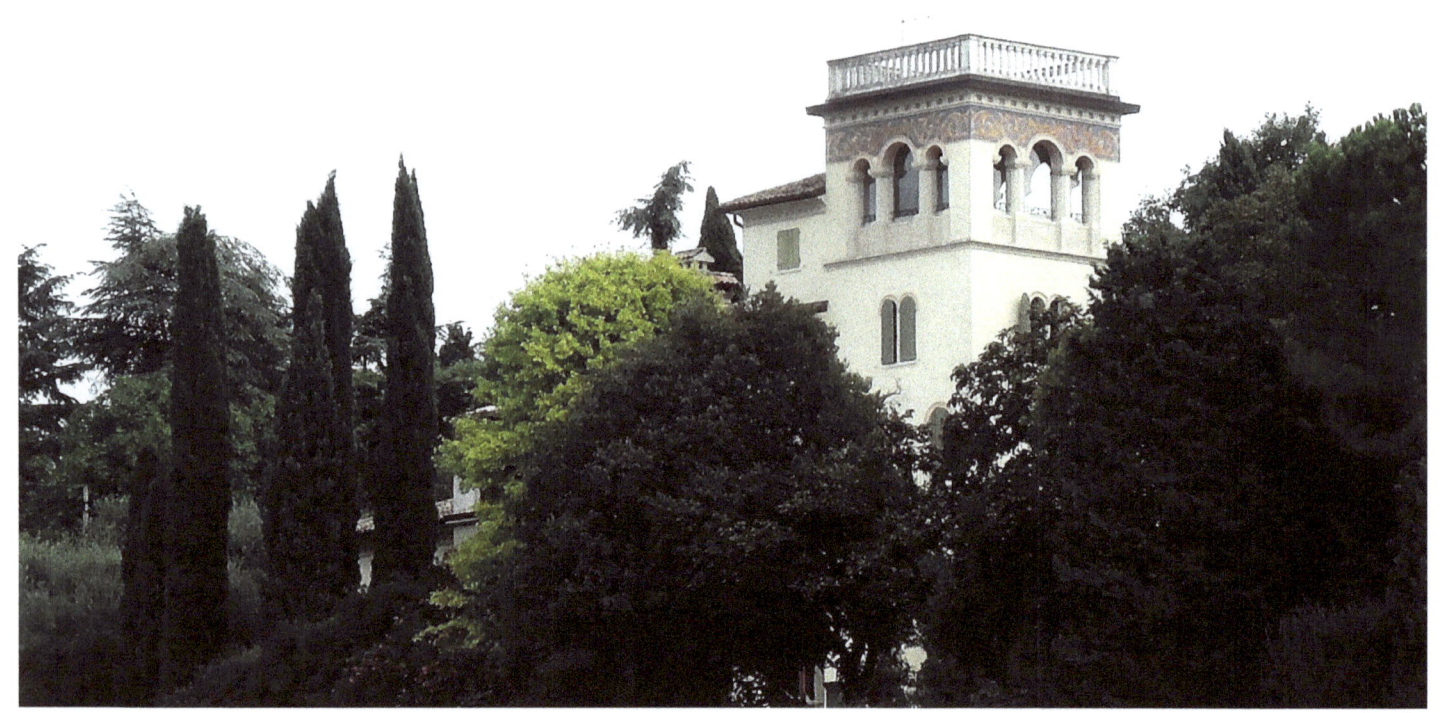
Asolo

Risotto con rigaglie, risotto with giblets. Chop the chicken giblets and put them to flavour in the sliced icing onion and sauté in the butter. Let them brown for about half an hour over a low heat, then add the rice, toast it and add the wine. Soften and proceed with cooking adding the hot stock with ladles. When the rice is al dente, add salt and season with freshly ground pepper and finely chopped parsley. Add a large knob of butter and a generous handful of grated cheese. Cover the pot and let sit for a few seconds then serve hot on the table.

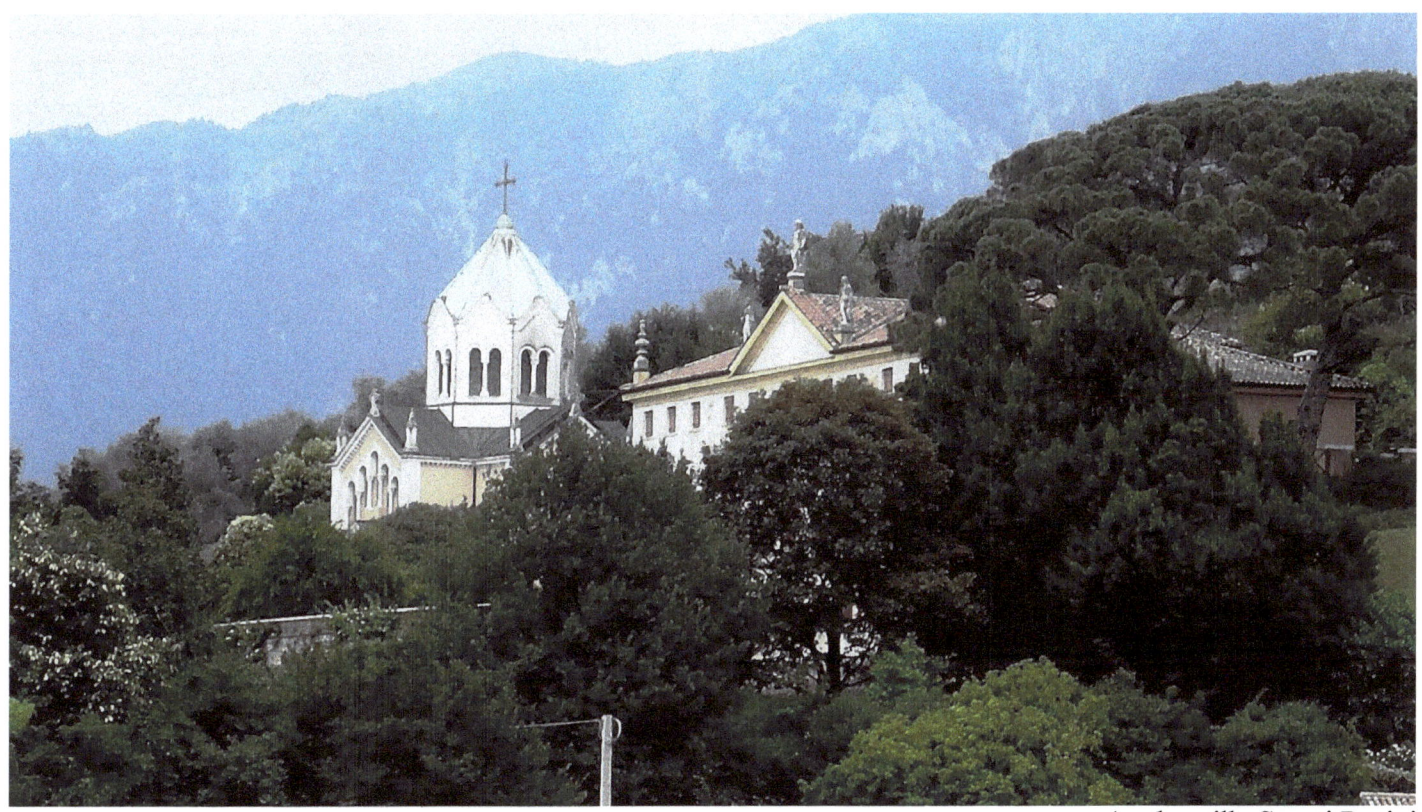

Asolo, villa Scotti Pasini

Zuppa di trippa, tripe soup. Repeatedly wash the tripe (bovine stomach) in water acidulated with lemon juice, then cut it into thin strips 3-4 cm long. Put it in a large pan without adding any seasoning and brown it for a few minutes. Remove the water formed during cooking and let it dry completely, stirring, over medium heat. Cut the leek into thin slices after dividing it in half lengthwise. Chop the celery, carrot and cabbage into short julienne strips. Make all wilt in a pan with a few tablespoons of oil, the aromatic bunch and the clove of garlic divided in half. Add the tripe, stir for a few minutes over a moderate heat, then remove the garlic and the aromatic bunch. Add salt and pepper, add the broth, cover and cook for about an hour (or even longer if the tripe is still hard), adding more broth if the soup is too dry. When cooked, add the chopped parsley.

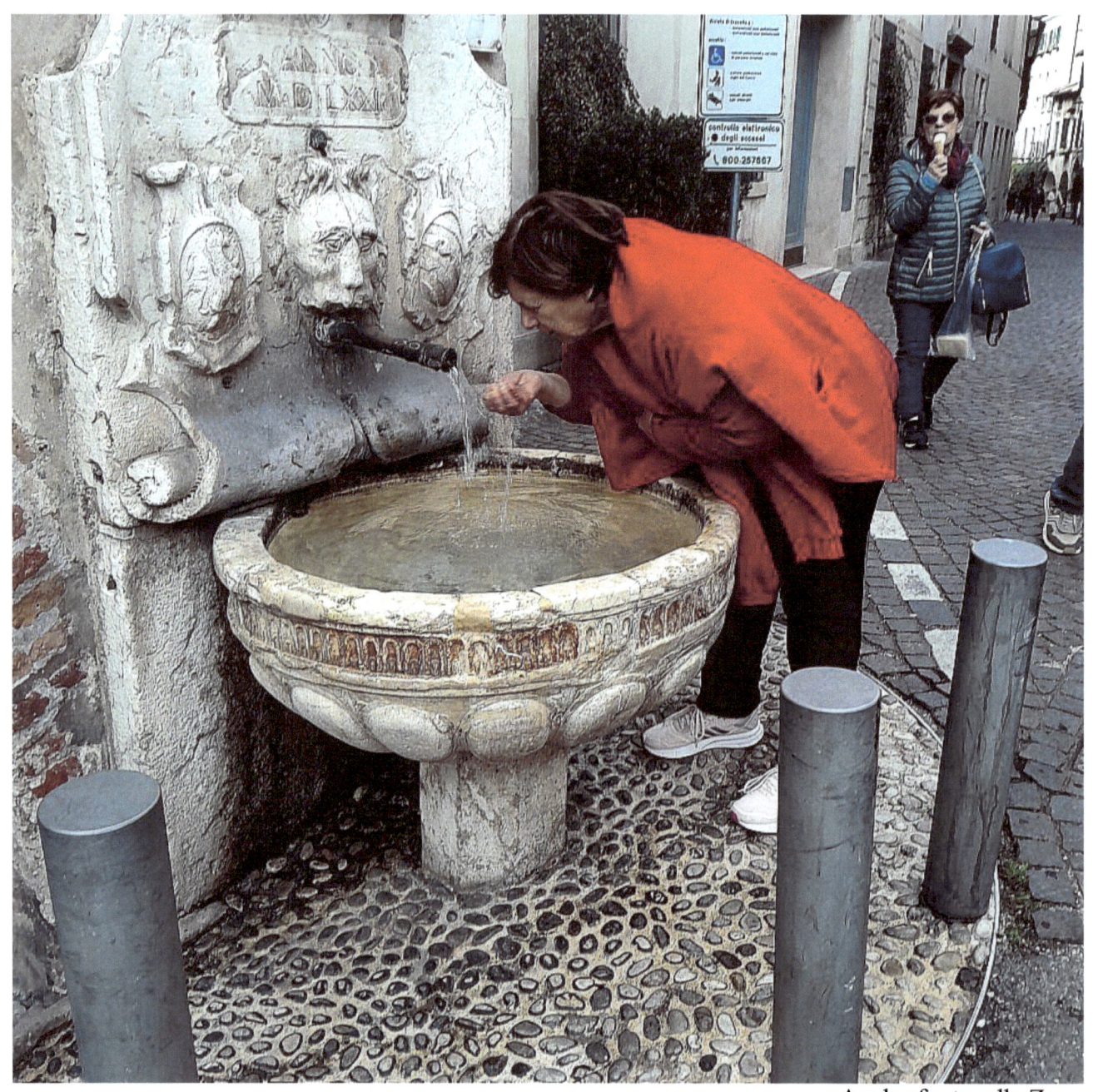

Asolo, fontanella Zen

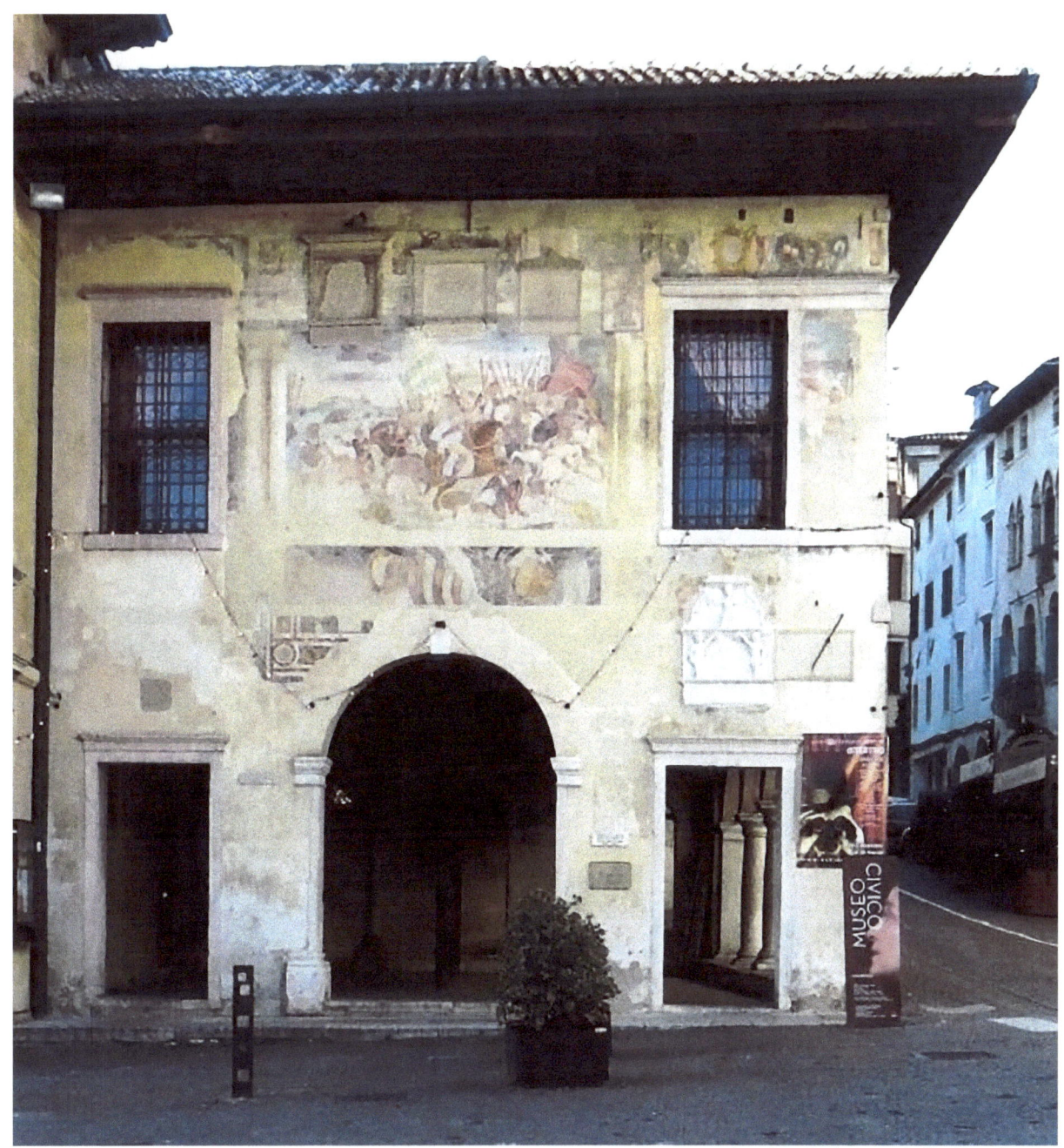

Asolo, Palazzo della Ragione

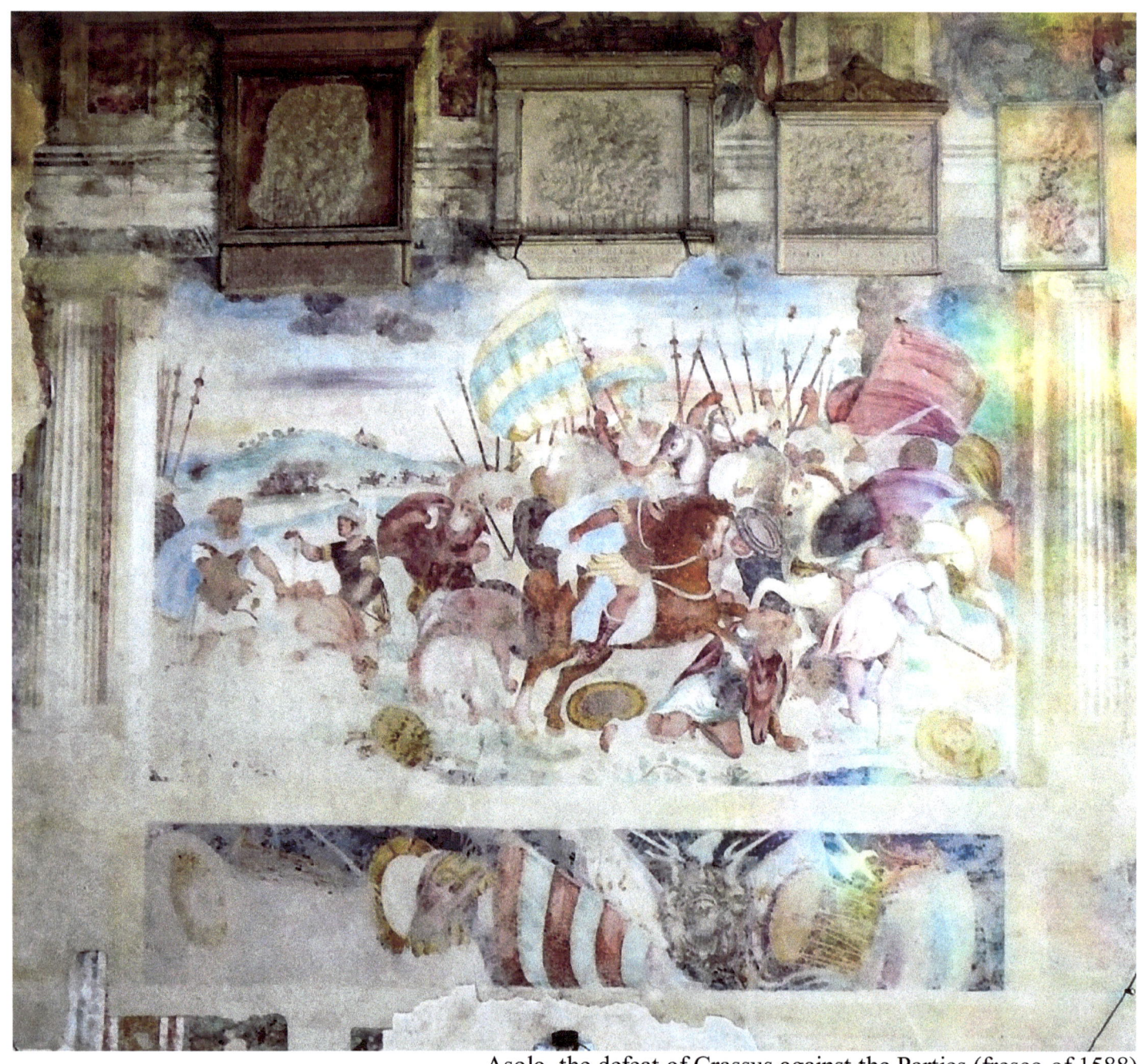

Asolo, the defeat of Crassus against the Parties (fresco of 1588)

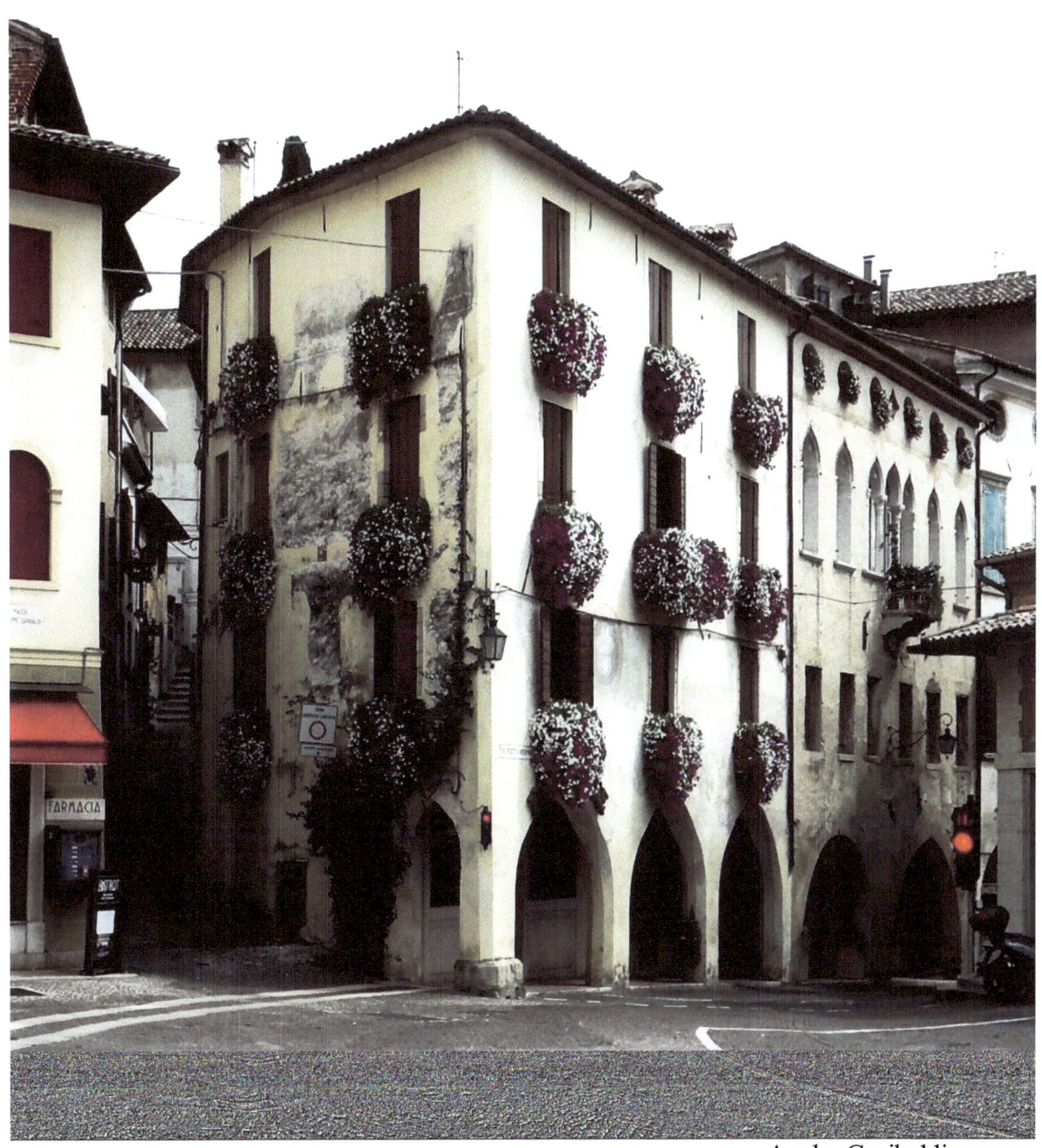
Asolo, Garibaldi square

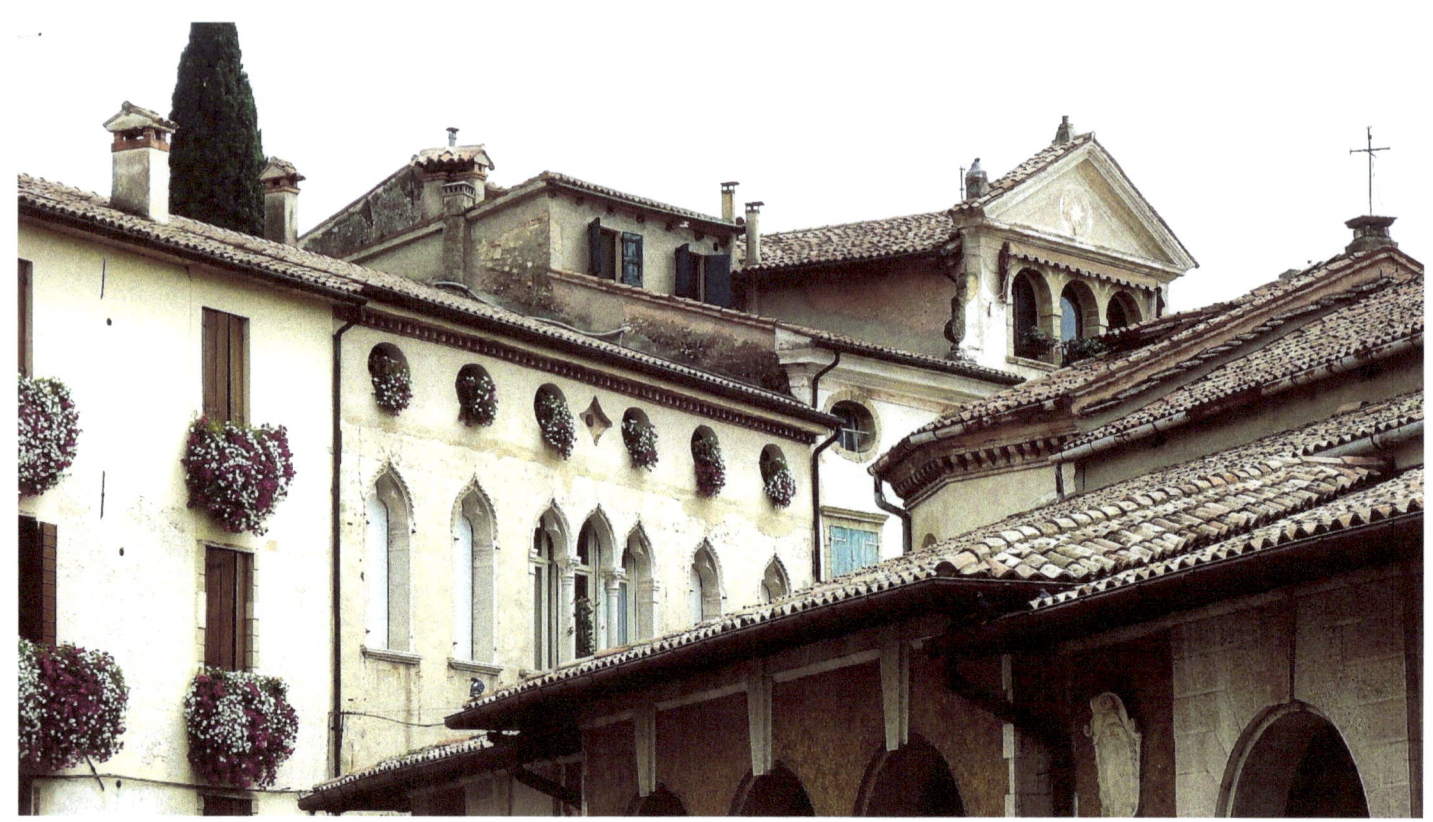
Asolo

Cappone in umido, capon stewed. Wash the capon pieces in water and place without draining them well in a pan. Let them cook uncovered for about 10 minutes without adding anything. In the meantime, prepare a mince with carrot, celery and onion, cover the bottom of a pan with oil and fry the chopped mixture. After a minute add the pieces of capon with salt and pepper, and brown them well on each side, turning them with a wooden spoon. Pour a glass of red wine and let it evaporate, to add the tomato puree at the end. Let simmer uncovered for about an hour, adding a few tablespoons of water if necessary to help cooking.

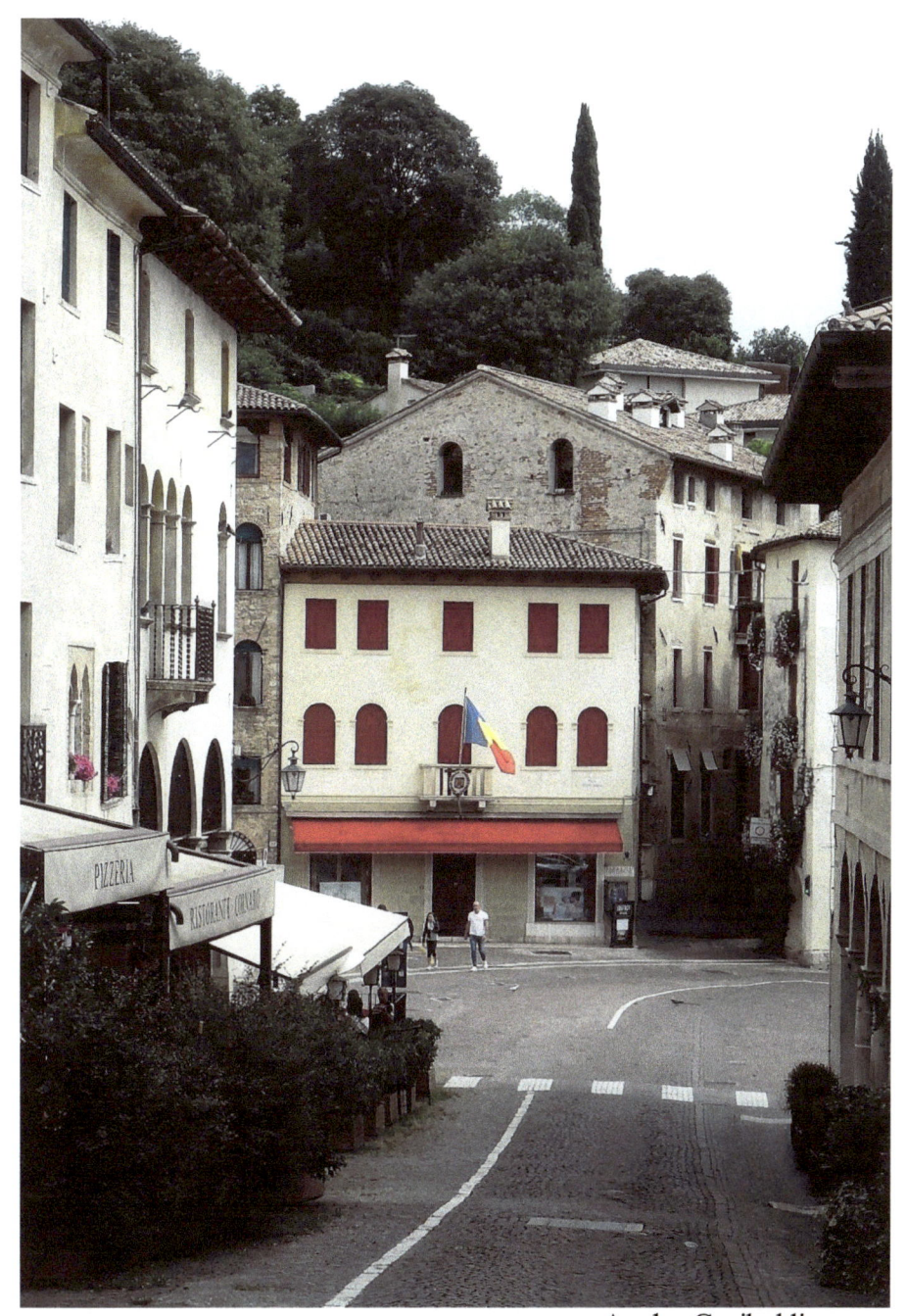

Asolo, Garibaldi square

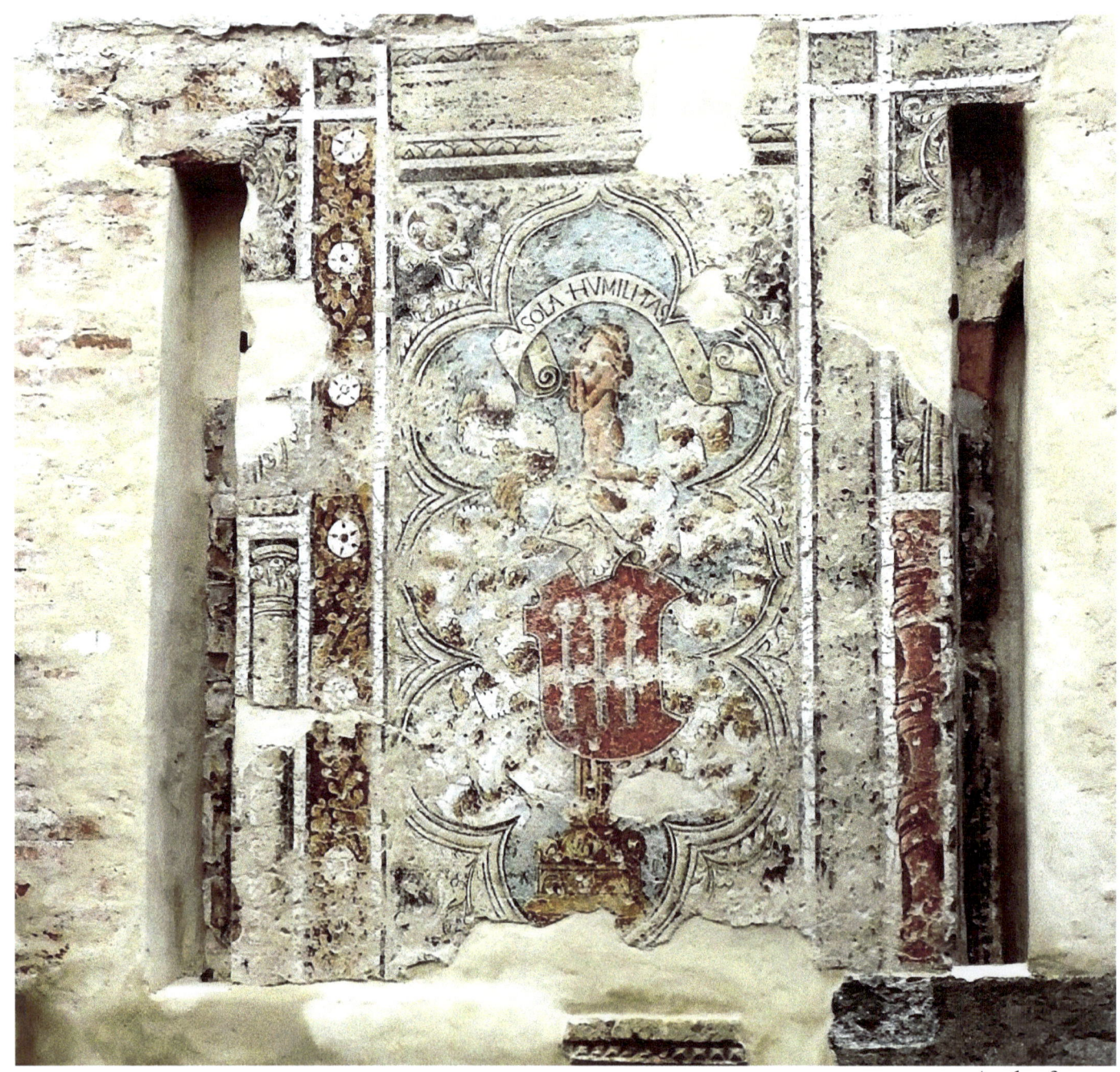

Asolo, fresco

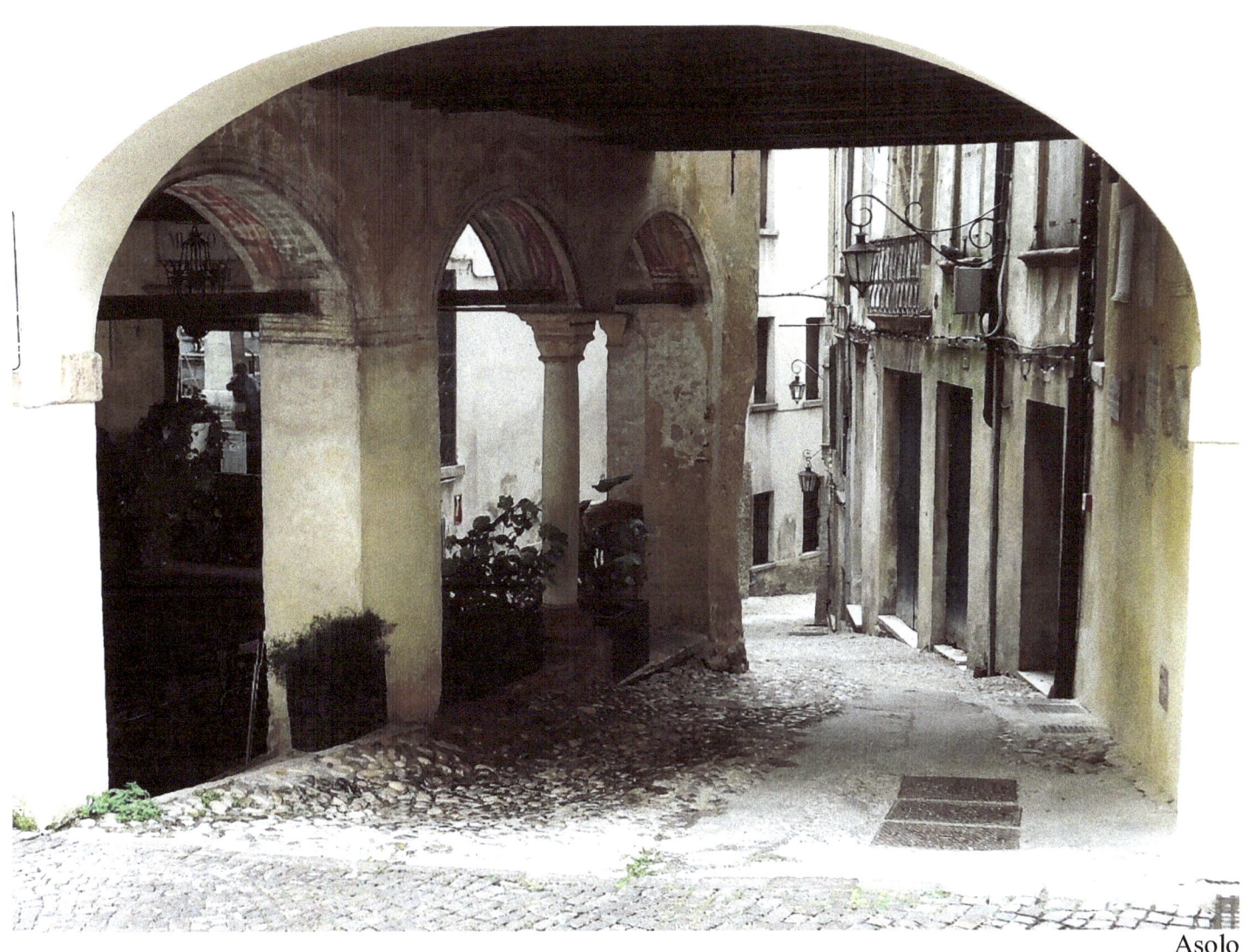
Asolo

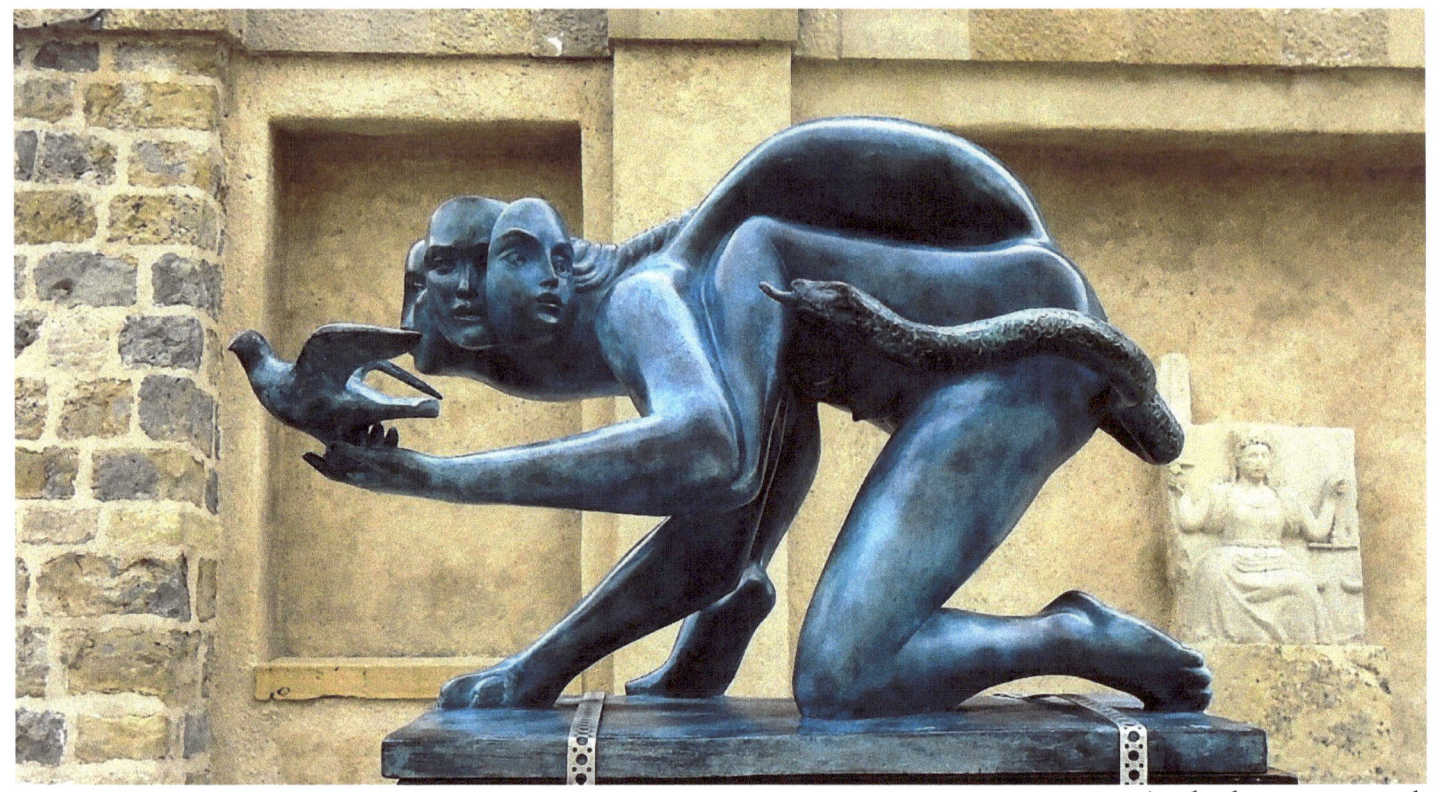

Asolo, bronze artwork

Fegato alla veneta, Venetian-style liver. A dish with different variations, but the base is always the same: excellent quality liver and onions. The most famous is the liver of Vicenza, which differs from one of Venice in the use of white wine instead of wine vinegar. Peel the onions and slice them thinly, melt the butter in a pan with the oil and simmer the onions with a pinch of salt, which they will have to slowly wither, without taking color. Peel the liver, removing the skin that covers it and the blood vessels, and cut it into strips about 3 mm thick. Raise the heat of the pan with the onions already cooked and sauté the liver, blending with the wine for about 5 minutes with a laurel leaf. Quick cooking will keep the liver soft. At the end, season with salt and pepper, and serve the hot venetian liver. If you wish, you can accompany the dish with a white corn polenta.

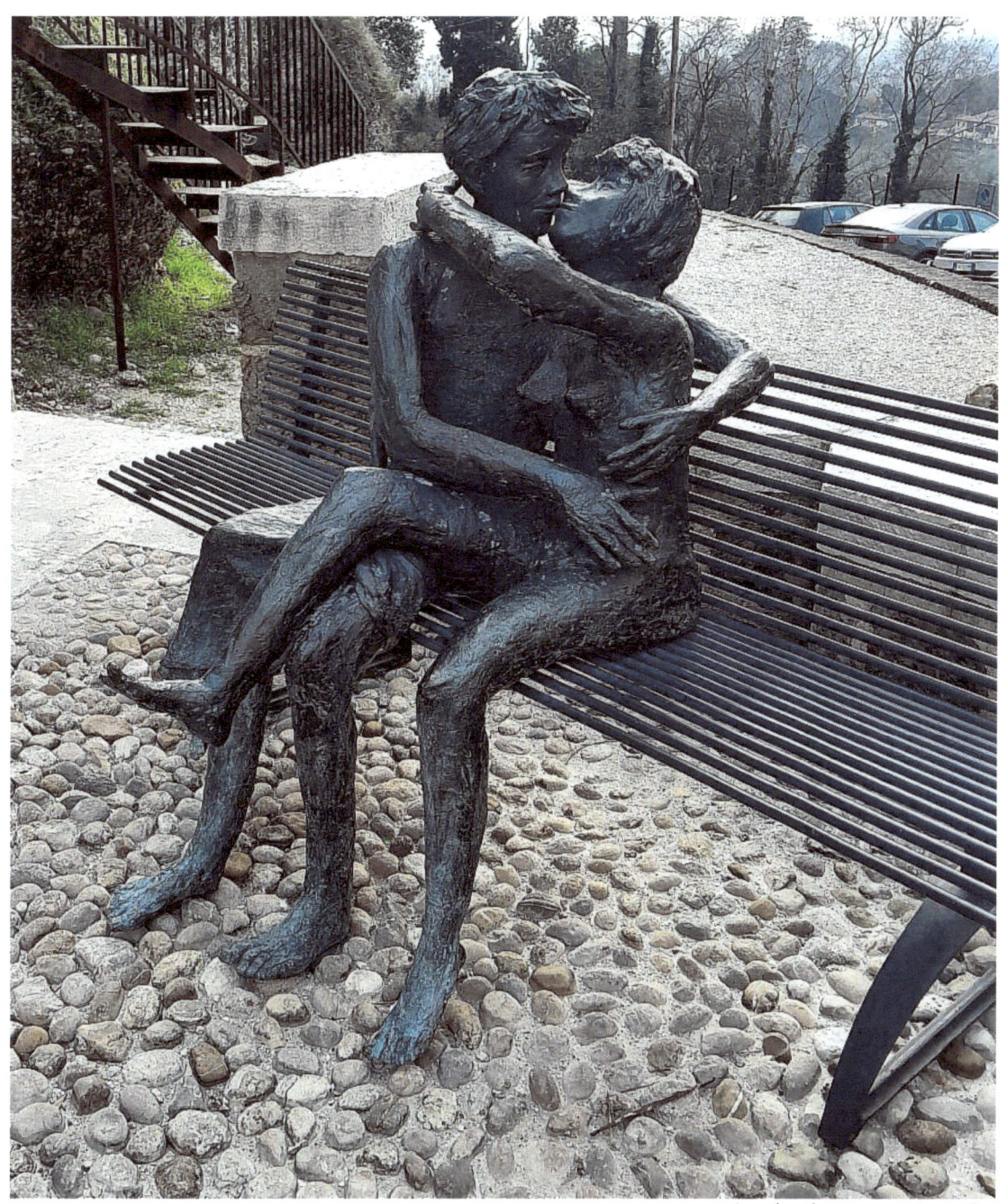

Asolo, bronze artwork

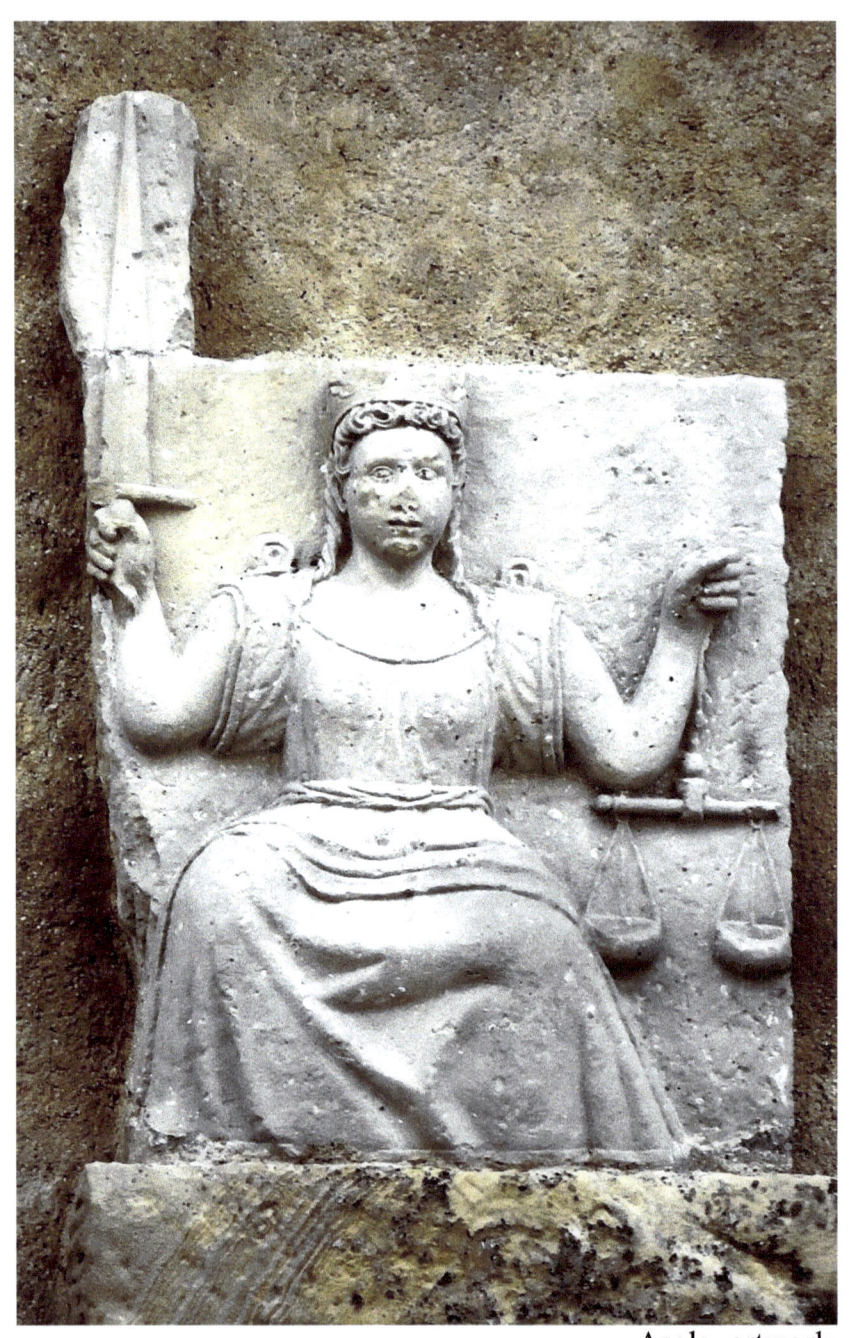

Asolo, artwork

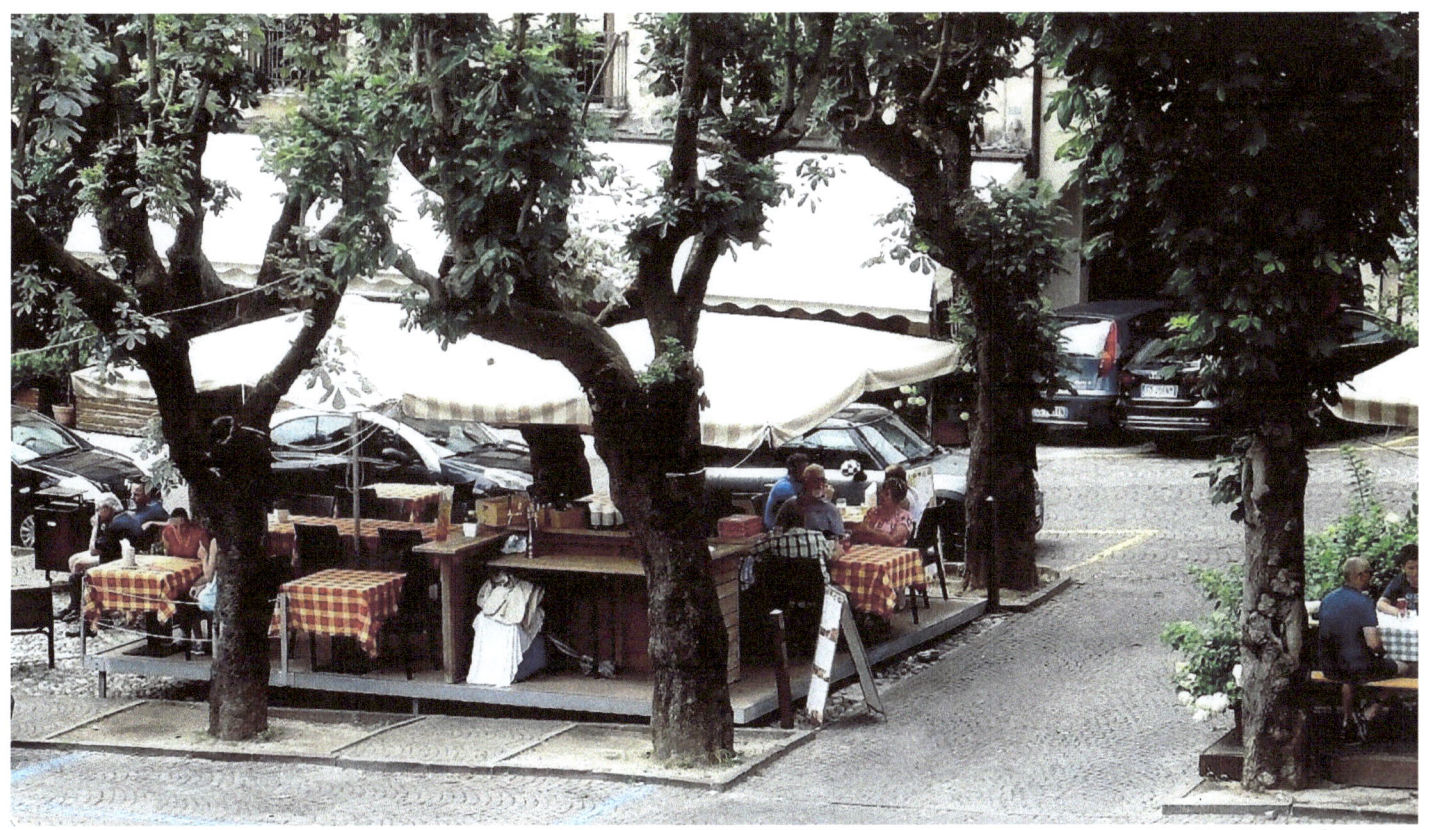

Asolo, Central square

Fritata coi bruscandoi, omelette with hop shoots. The bruscandoli are the vegetative apexes of wild Hops that sprout spontaneously in our countryside between March and May. Their flavor is firm, slightly bitter and goes perfectly with eggs. Clean the bruscandoli and boil them in boiling salted water for 4-5 minutes, then drain and let them cool. Peel the onion and cut it finely. Heat the butter with the oil and half an onion in a non-stick pan and sauté over low heat. When it is well wilted add the bruscandoli and let them season for about ten minutes. Meanwhile shell the eggs in a bowl, add salt and whisk well with a fork. While stirring, add three tablespoons of milk, baking powder and finally the grated Parmesan. When the bruscandoli are ready and still hot, pour in the egg mixture. Let the omelette firm up, then with the help of a lid or a plate turn it and then slide it back into the pan to cook it on the other side. When it is well browned on both sides, serve it hot.

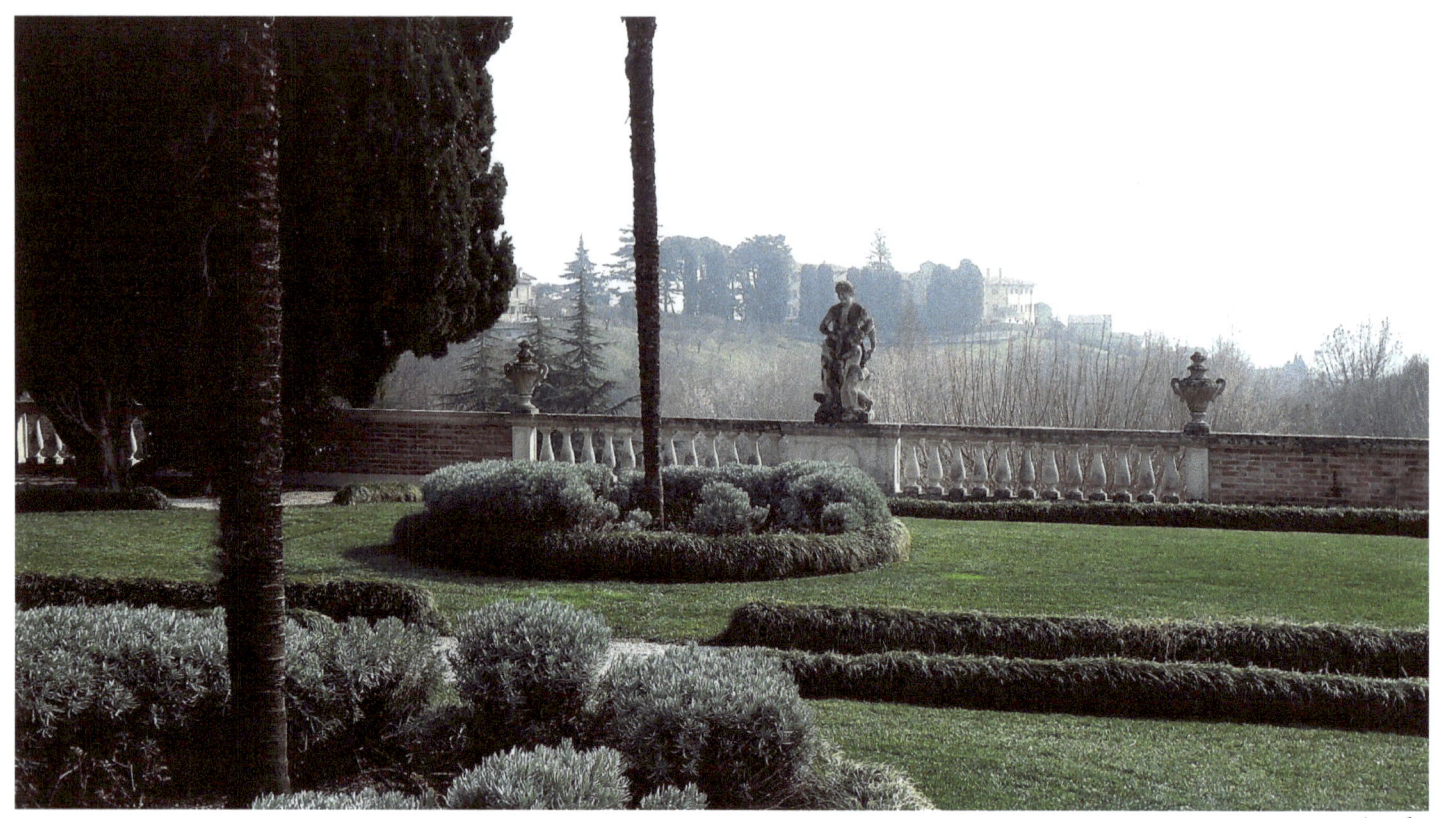
Asolo

Gran bollito misto alla veneta, great boiled meat mixed Venetian-style. The mixed boiled meat is usually made up of at least four cuts, even better if there are seven, choosing at will between beef, cotechino, tongue, calf's head, hen, loin, tail and paw. Inside a pot, add the cuts of beef and the cold water, wait for the temperature to rise and remove the impurities with the skimmer. Now you can add the celery, carrot and onion in chunks with a pinch of salt. Follow the same procedure for the tongue in another pot, except that the skin is removed when cooked. The same for cotechino, but without carrots and salt. Strain the broth of beef and one of hen, whereas the cotechino cooking water is discarded because it is too fat. A good boiled meat should never boil because the meat would become stringy while maintaining very light cooking, barely hinting at the movement of the liquid. At the end of cooking slice the meat and accompany it with cooked seasonal herbs or mashed potatoes, green sauce, horseradish and Venetian mustard.

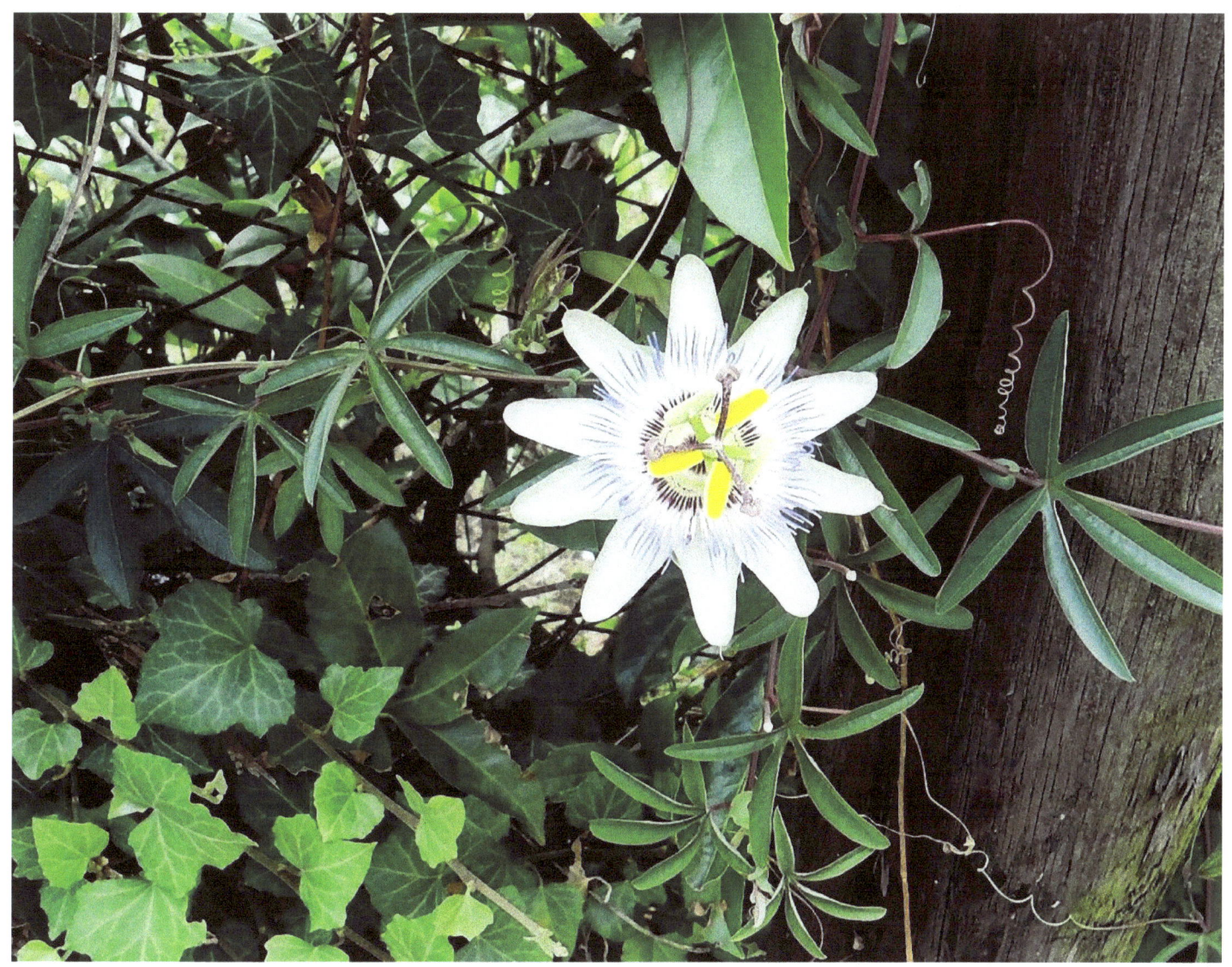
Asolo

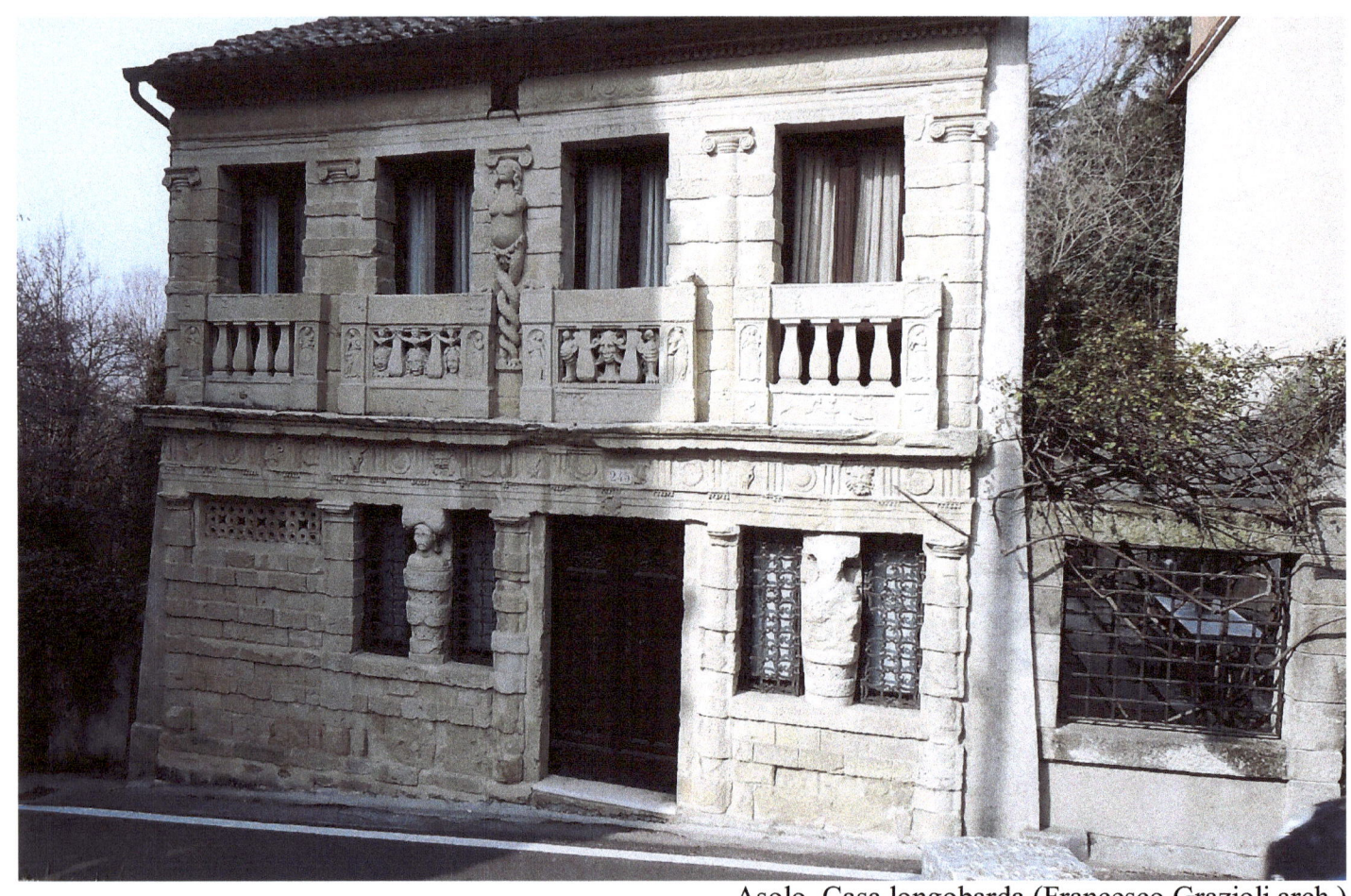

Asolo, Casa longobarda (Francesco Grazioli arch.)

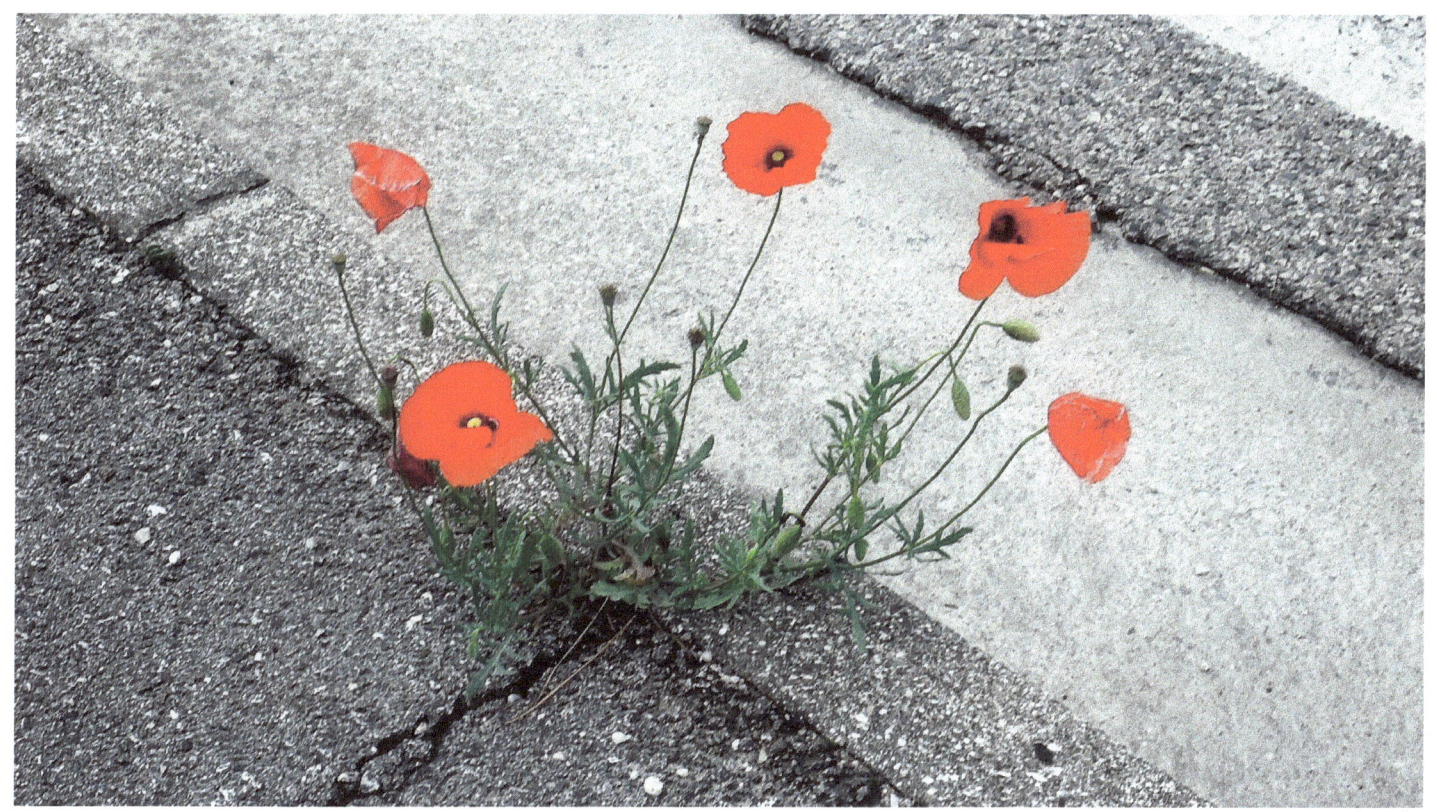
Asolo

Lepre in umido con polenta, hare stewed with polenta. Cut the hare into pieces and marinate them in wine with garlic cloves, juniper berries, bay leaves, rosemary, salt, pepper and red wine to cover the meat. Let them rest for about 12 hours in the marinade, stirring occasionally. Put a saucepan with three tablespoons of oil, lard, rosemary, garlic and pepper on the heat. Add the pieces of hare and the coarse salt so that its water comes out, emptying it as it comes out, until the pieces of meat are dry. At this point the hare is ready for cooking. Fry the pieces of hare until they have a nice golden color. Sprinkle with the wine from the marinade and let it evaporate. Add the tomatoes, tomato puree and broth, when necessary, and cook for about two hours, stirring occasionally. Put the hare in the serving dish and pour the sauce over it. Serve hot with polenta.

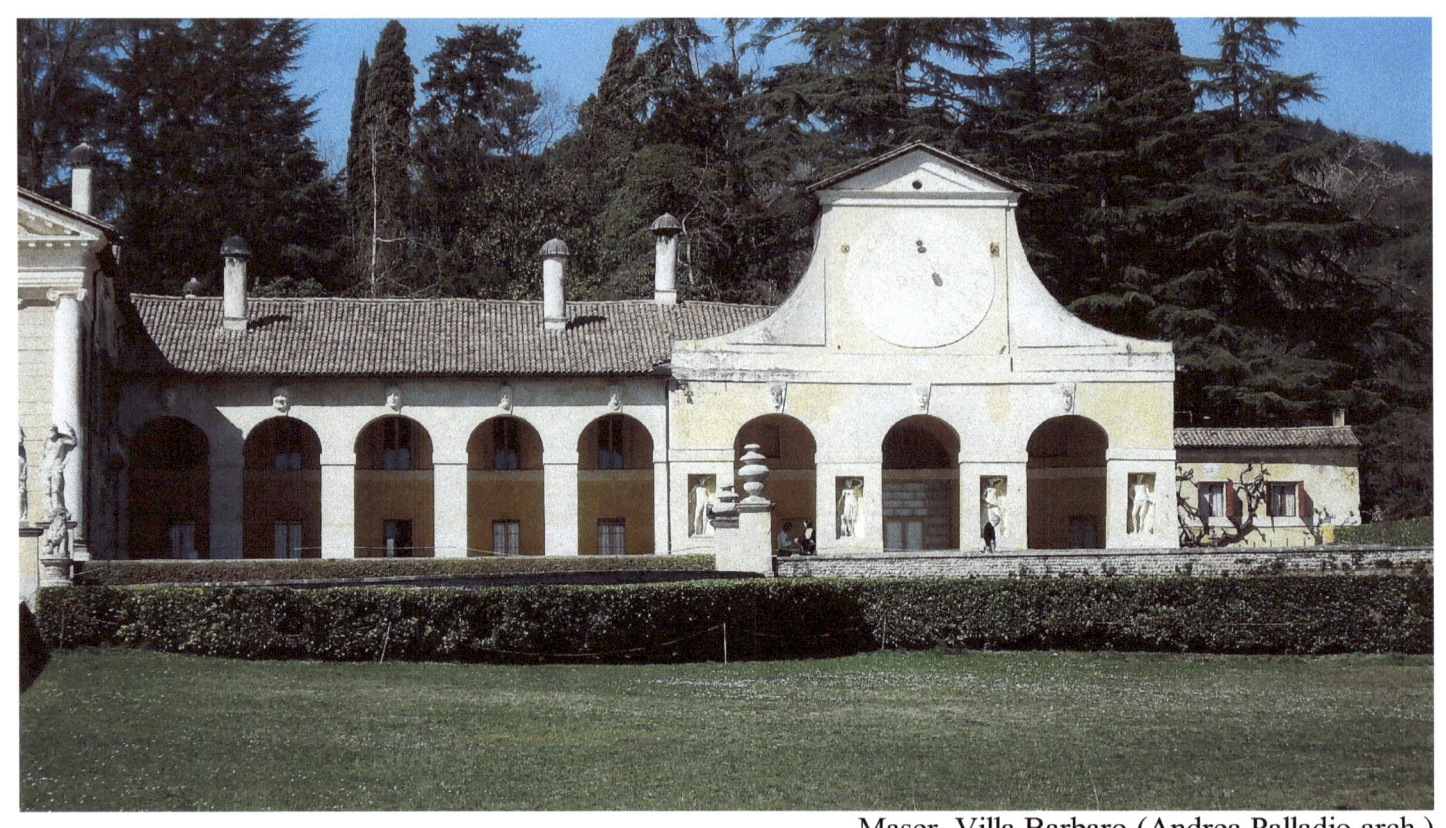

Maser, Villa Barbaro (Andrea Palladio arch.)

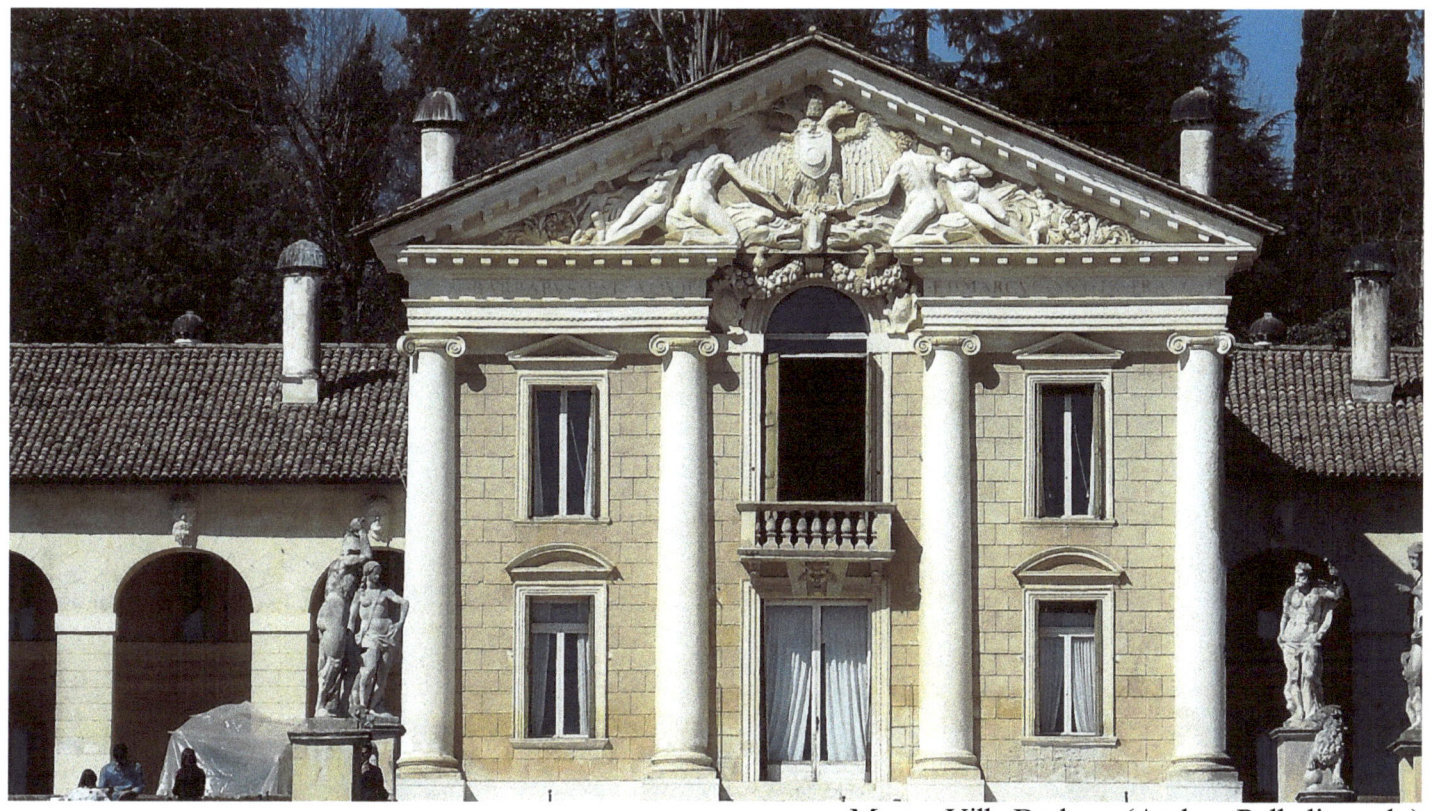

Maser, Villa Barbaro (Andrea Palladio arch.)

Lumache in umido, snails stewed. Dip the snails in boiling water, cook them for about ten minutes, drain and remove them from the shell, using a pair of shellfish tweezers or even a toothpick. Clean them by removing the intestine and wash them several times with water and vinegar. After that rub them with yellow flour, salt and vinegar. Wash them again with water and vinegar and dry one by one with a cloth or leave to drain in a colander. Prepare a piece of onion and fry it in plenty of butter and oil, adding some pieces of lard. Then add the snails and brown them adding a mixture of garlic, parsley and peeled tomatoes. Sprinkle with a ladle of hot water and cook for about an hour and a half, adding the salt before bringing to the table.

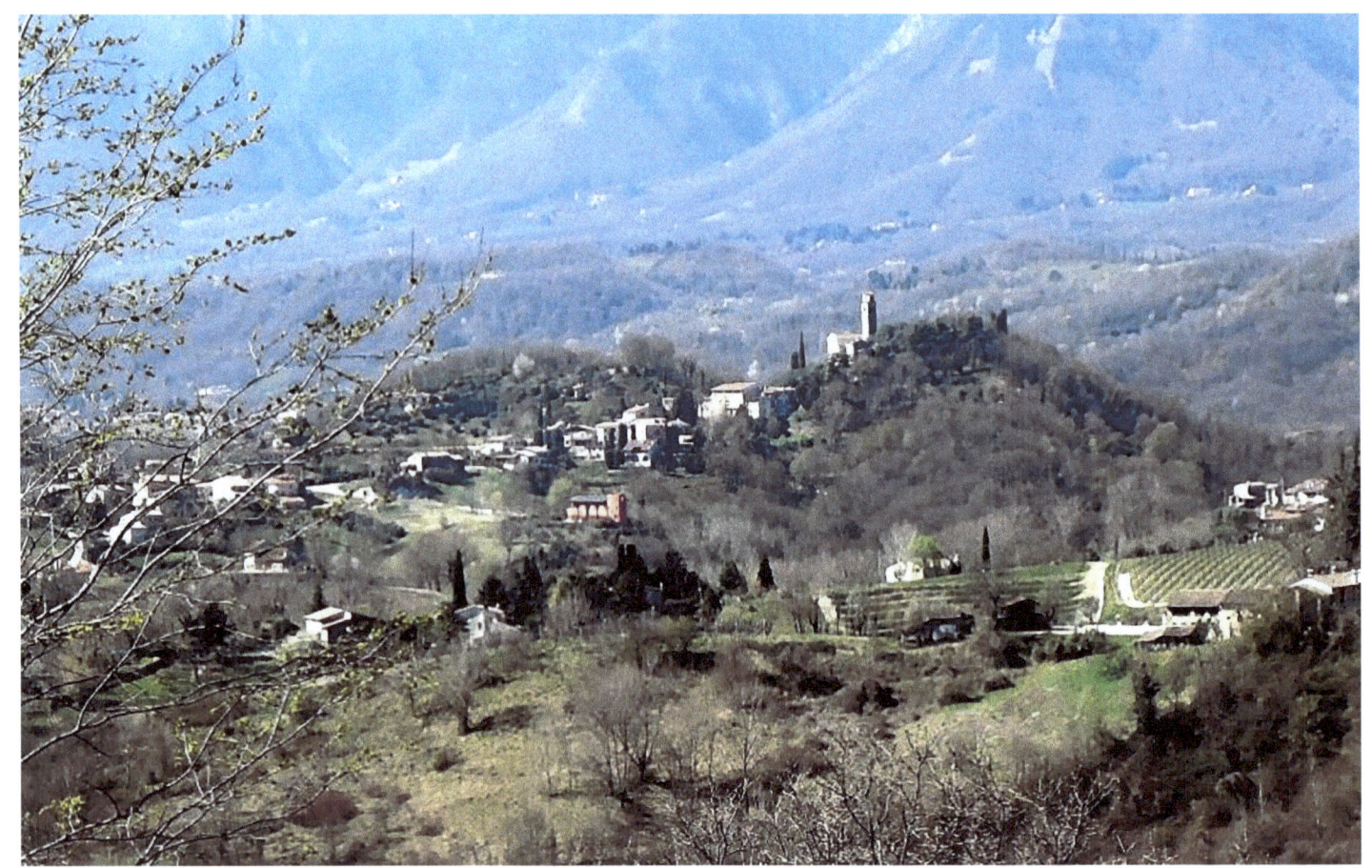
Monfumo

Oca in onto, goose in cooking fat. Take off neck, legs, wings and all the innards of a nice big goose. Clean it well, cut it into pieces and place it in a deep saucepan, with olive oil, a glass of water, salt, rosemary, sage, and cook it in the oven with the lid on a very low heat for three hours. Collect all the fat, boned the goose pieces and place them in a pan with laurel leaves covering them with their cooking fat. Cover the pot with parchment and tie the opening. The goose thus treated will be a reserve of meat for the whole winter and the fat will be an excellent condiment for tagliatelle, especially in combination with peas.

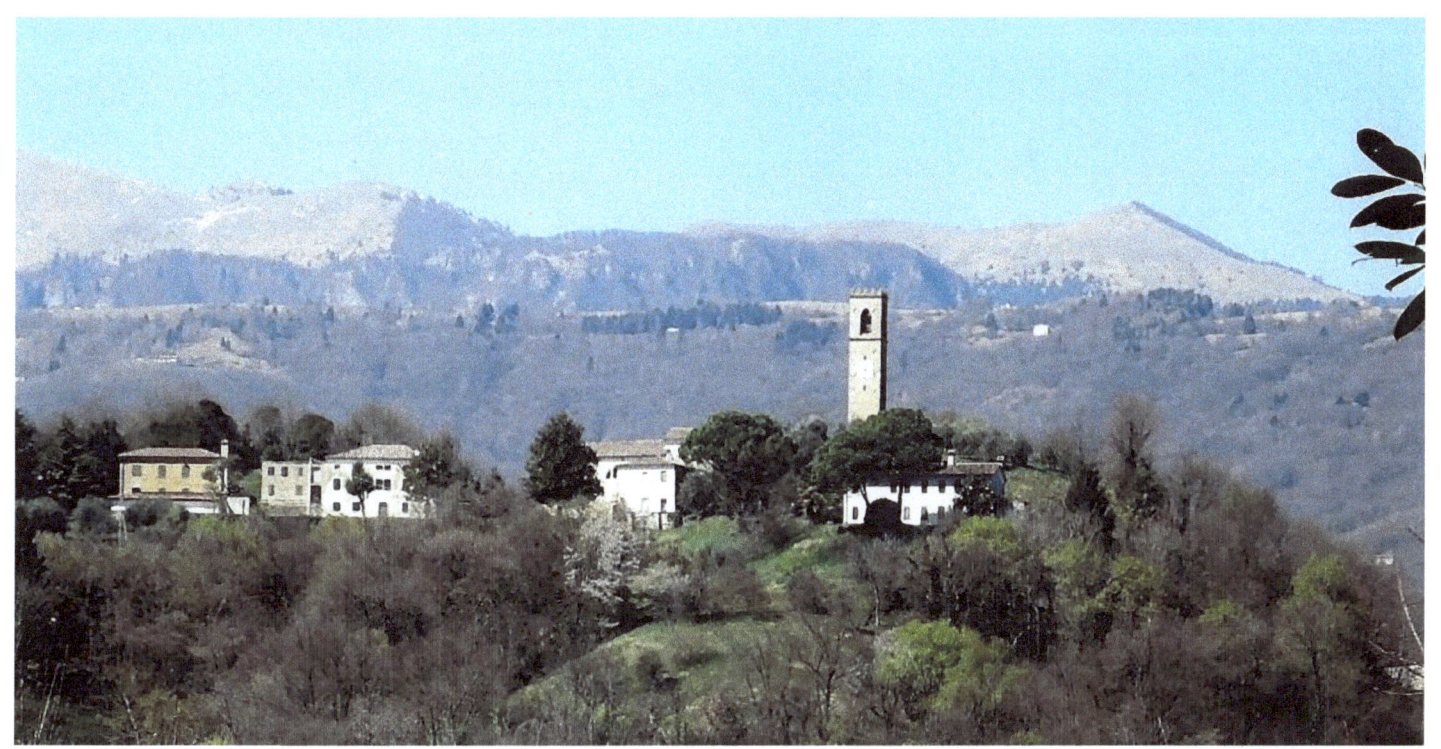
San Giorgio in Castelli church (Monfumo)

Polastro in tecia, chicken in pot. Clean, empty, flame, wash and dry the chicken, then cut it into pieces. Fry a chopped vegetable (onion, carrot, celery, garlic) in a saucepan with oil and add the bacon. Lightly brown it and place the chicken pieces that you will brown. Add salt and pepper, sprinkle with dry white wine and let it evaporate over high heat. Then add the rosemary, sage and chopped tomatoes. Cover and cook for half an hour on a low heat. Season with salt, add the chopped parsley and serve the chicken with steaming polenta.

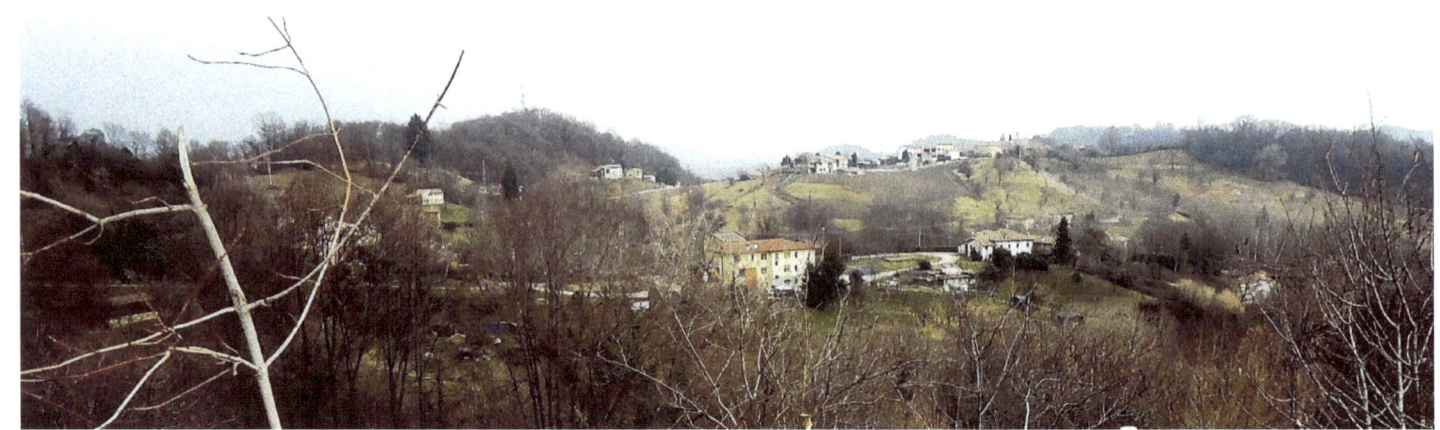
Bocca di Serra and Castelcies (Cavaso del Tomba)

Polenta e baccalà alla vicentina, polenta and cod Vicenza-style. Soak the cod (stockfish) for at least 24 hours in cold water, changing it often. Fry lightly with olive oil and thinly sliced onion, some sardines reduced to a pulp and a clove of garlic, which will be removed shortly afterwards. Peel the cod calmly, removing all the bones, cut it into pieces and fry them with the onion and sardines. Melt a tablespoon of white flour in half a liter of milk, pour it over the cod with a little chopped parsley and sprinkle with plenty of grated parmesan. Put the pan to cook over very low heat for at least four hours, stirring gently every so often. Season with salt and pepper. Baccalà alla vicentina should always be served with white polenta.

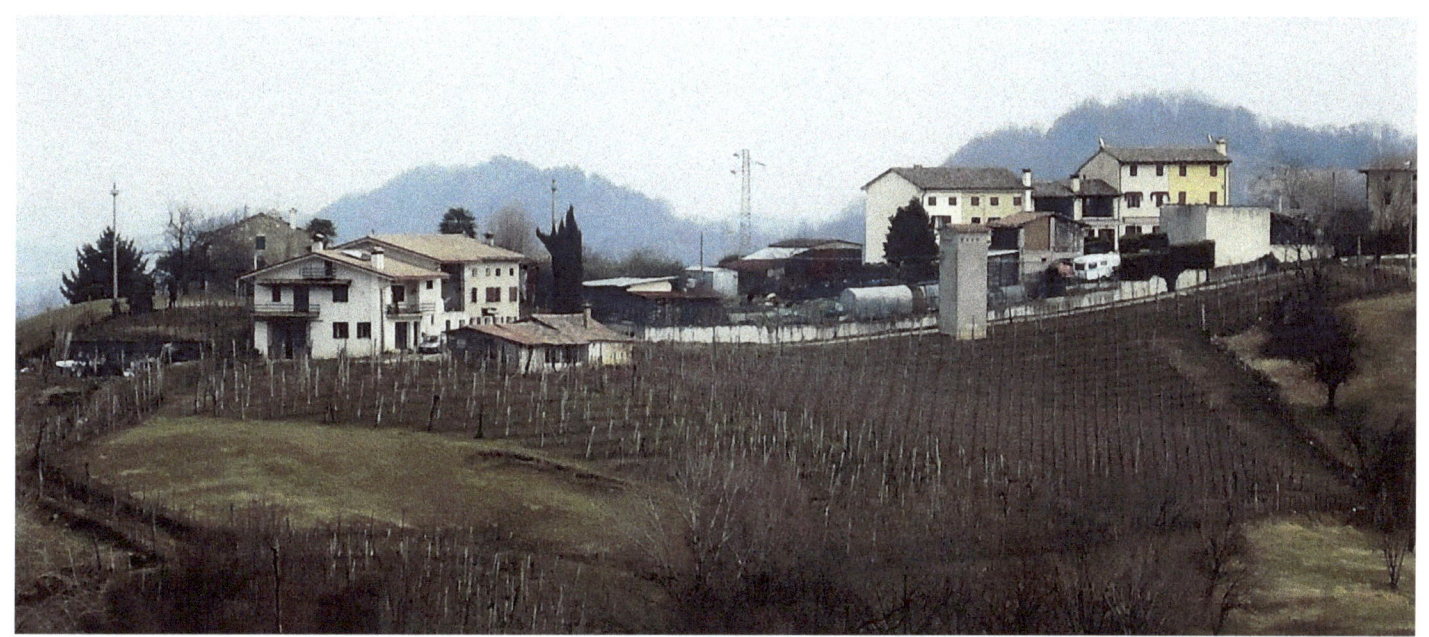

Castelcies (Cavaso del Tomba)

Poenta e osei, polenta and birds. Typical Venetian recipe based on polenta and small birds, in particular beccafichi, larks, thrushes or robins, cooked on a spit on the fireplace or in a pan, and seasoned with lard, butter and sage. For the preparation of polenta e osei, use coarse-grained corn flour. To soften the smell of the game, add some bay leaves and juniper berries. Cook the birds over a low heat, turning them from time to time to make them brown evenly: they are in fact birds with very thin skin that can easily burn. If the game meat is too dry, add some more butter. Avoid adding water or broth, otherwise the meat may then be tasteless. Instead of lard you can also use bacon, the meat will be softer and even tastier.

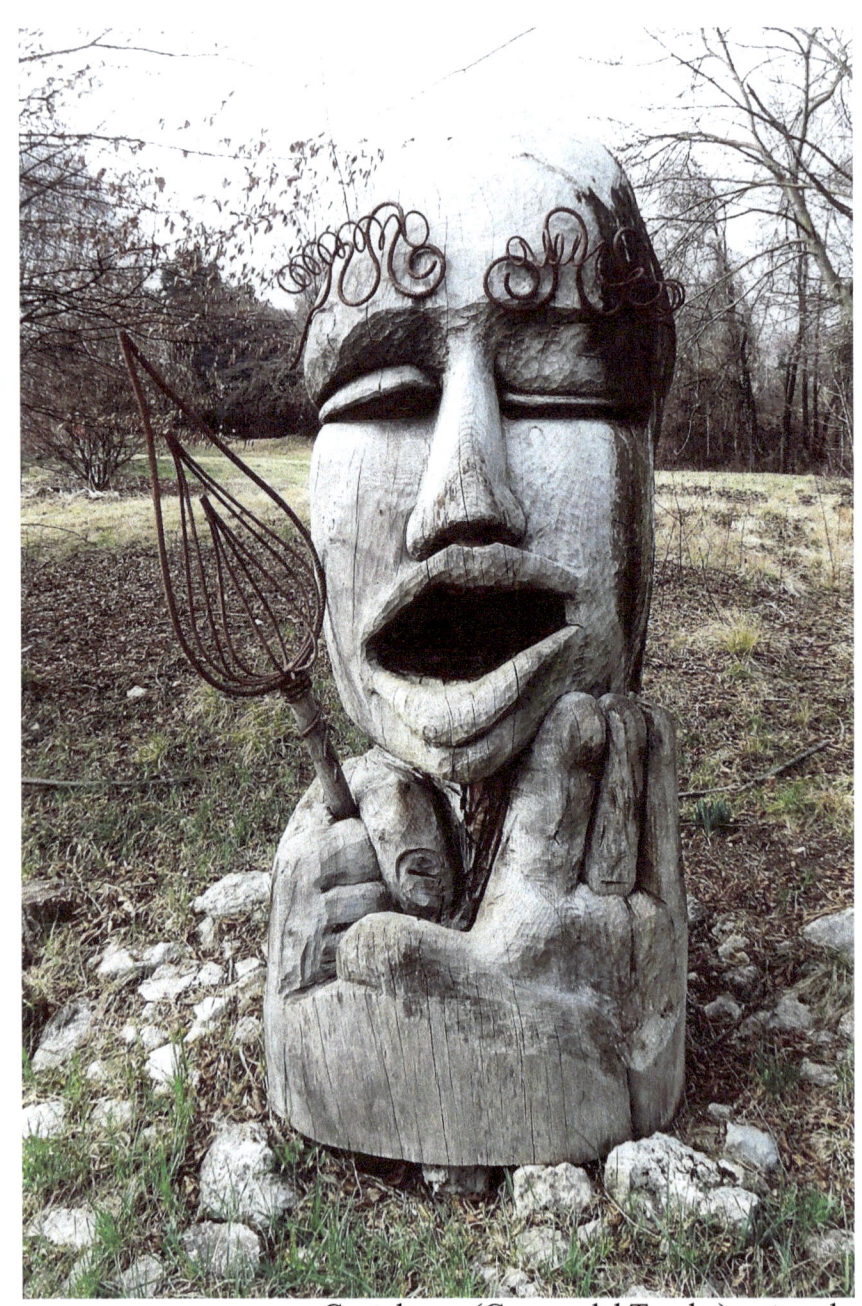
Costalunga (Cavaso del Tomba), artwork

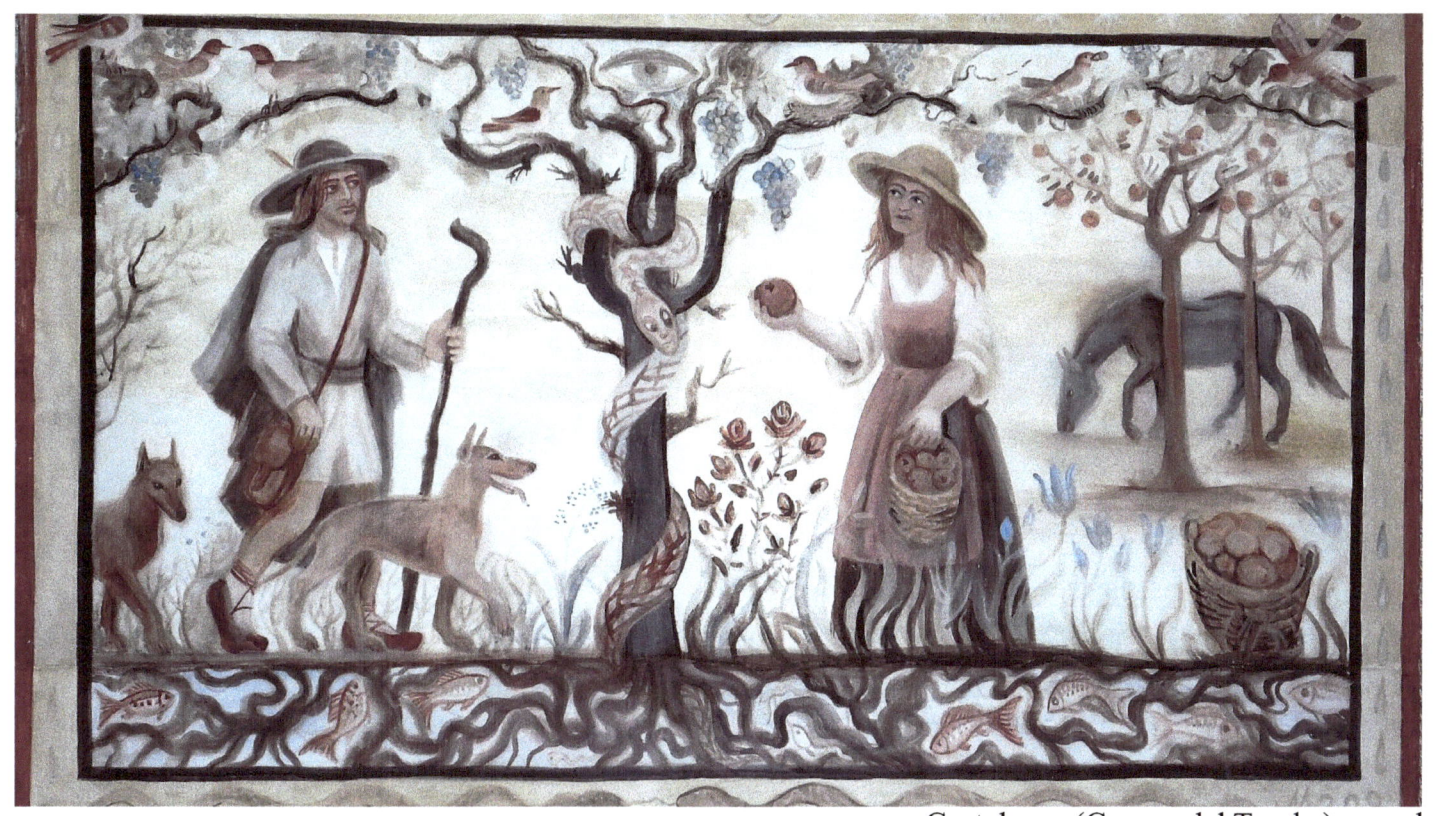

Costalunga (Cavaso del Tomba), mural

Crema fritta alla veneta, fried Venetian-style cream. Thoroughly wash a lemon and peel it with a potato peeler. Pour half a liter of milk into a saucepan, add the lemon zest and bring to a boil. In a bowl, beat 2 whole eggs and 2 egg yolks, add the sugar and mix. Add a pound of flour and 15 gr. of cornstarch continuing to whisk until a lump-free compound is obtained. Remove the pan from the heat, remove the lemon zest and pour in the egg cream. Stir and bring back on the heat to very low heat, continuing to mix until the cream thickens. Remove the cream from the heat and let it cool by stirring it occasionally, then pour it into a baking pan lined with a sheet of film. Level it with a spatula and let it cool completely. Once cooled let it thicken in the fridge for at least two hours. Beat two eggs in a bowl and bring plenty of seed oil. Cut the cream into diamonds and pass them in the beaten egg, then in the breadcrumbs and fry them in the oil until a golden and crispy crust is formed. Finally, place the fried cream on a sheet of absorbent paper to remove excess grease.

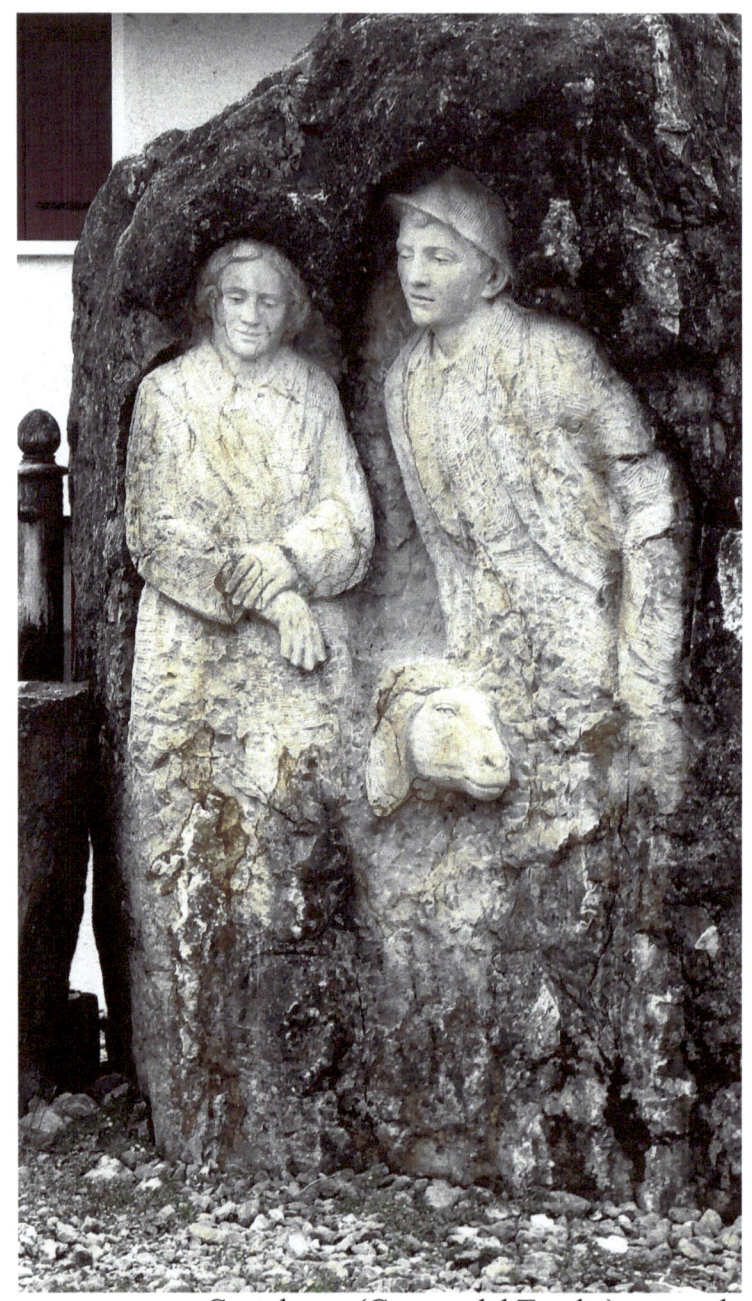

Costalunga (Cavaso del Tomba), artwork

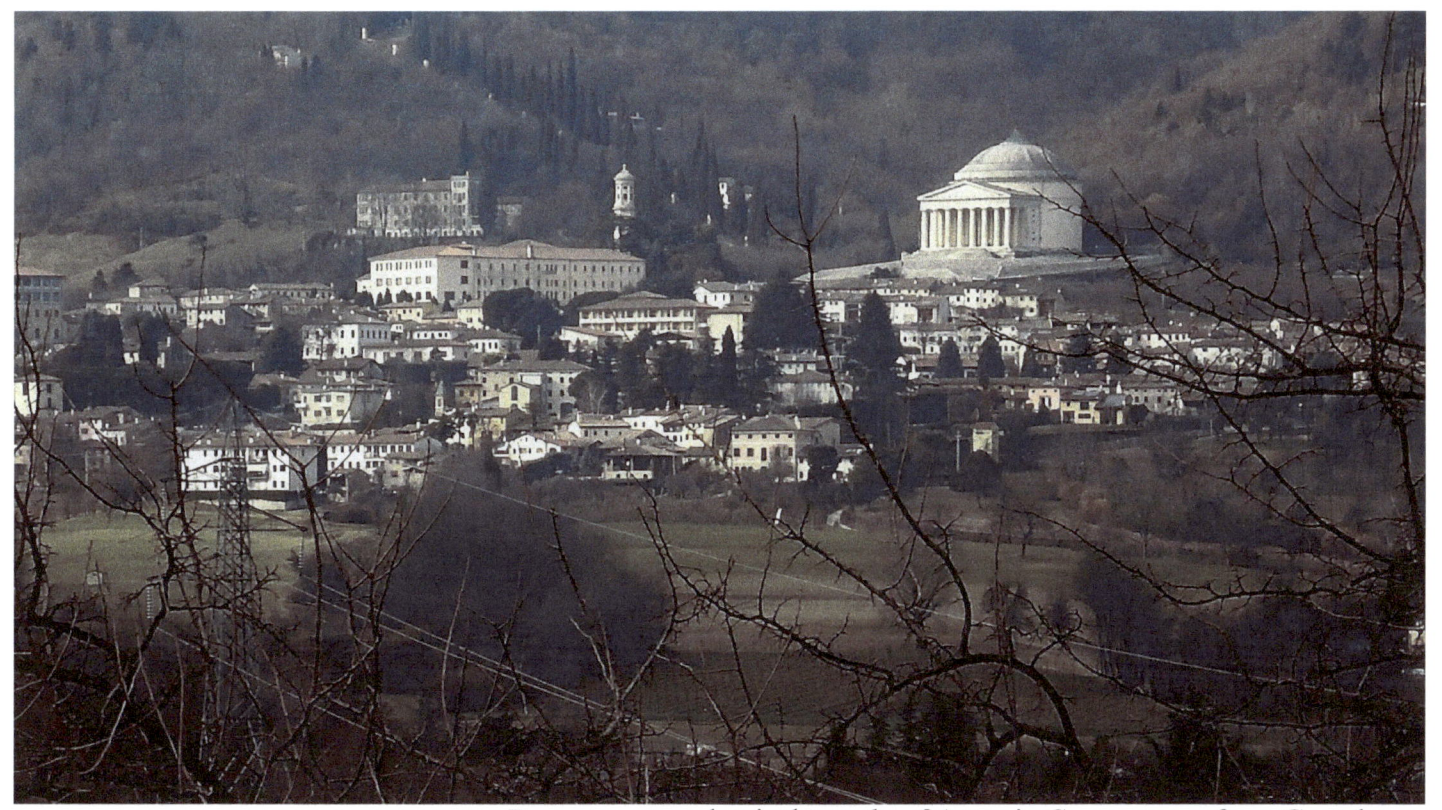
Possagno, neoclassical temple of Antonio Canova seen from Costalunga

Croccanti alle noci, crunchy with walnuts. Heat a thick-bottomed saucepan (preferably in copper) with sugar and two tablespoons of water over a gentle heat, stirring constantly until the whole is caramelized. Heat the oven slightly to warm the walnuts or sauté briefly in the pan and then rub them well in a cloth to remove excess skins. Add the lemon juice to the caramel and then the lukewarm walnuts. Pour everything onto a sheet of baking paper, leveling with a lightly oiled spatula. Let it cool and serve the crunchy cut into pieces.

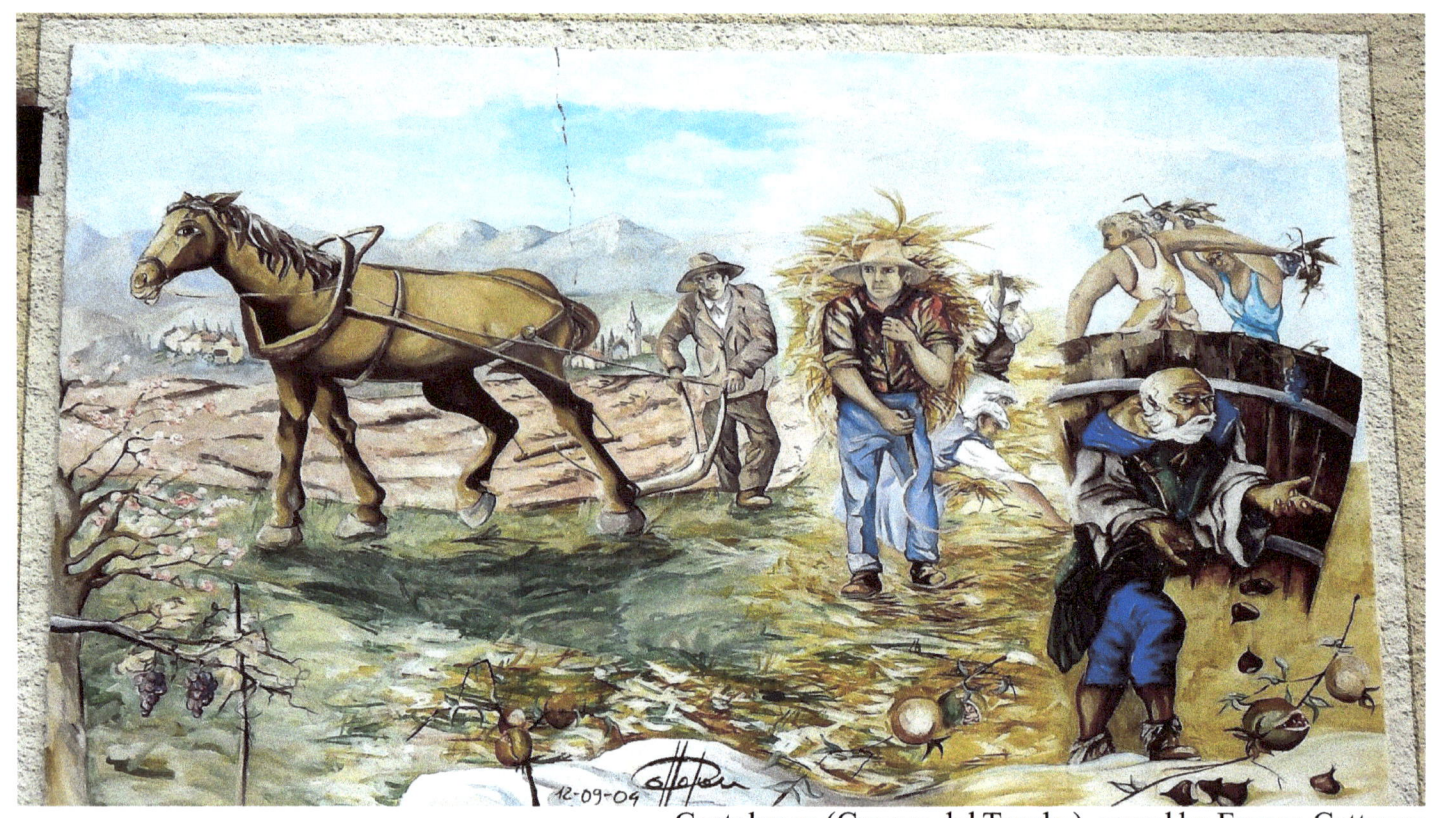

Costalunga (Cavaso del Tomba), mural by Franco Cattapan

Crostoi de Carnevae, crostoli of Carnival. In a bowl form a well with the flour, sugar and a pinch of salt and in the center add the butter, grappa and eggs. Start working the dough with a fork, starting from the center. When you have obtained a creamy dough, continue by hand, until you get a dough that comes off from the walls of the bowl (at least 15 minutes) until an elastic and homogeneous mass is obtained. Form a loaf, wrap it in cling film and let it rest for another 15 minutes at room temperature.

Divide the dough into 4 parts and roll it out one piece at a time, thinner than you can with a well-floured rolling pin and fold the dough over itself a couple of times, until a thin and homogeneous sheet is obtained. With a serrated cutter wheel cut it into rectangles or rhombuses, place them on a lightly floured surface and detached from each other. Fry the crostoli in abundant hot oil until they are golden brown and the classic bubbles will have formed. After a few seconds turn them and when they are golden brown take them with a slotted spoon and pass them on absorbent paper to dry the excess oil. Sprinkle the crostoli with plenty of icing sugar and serve.

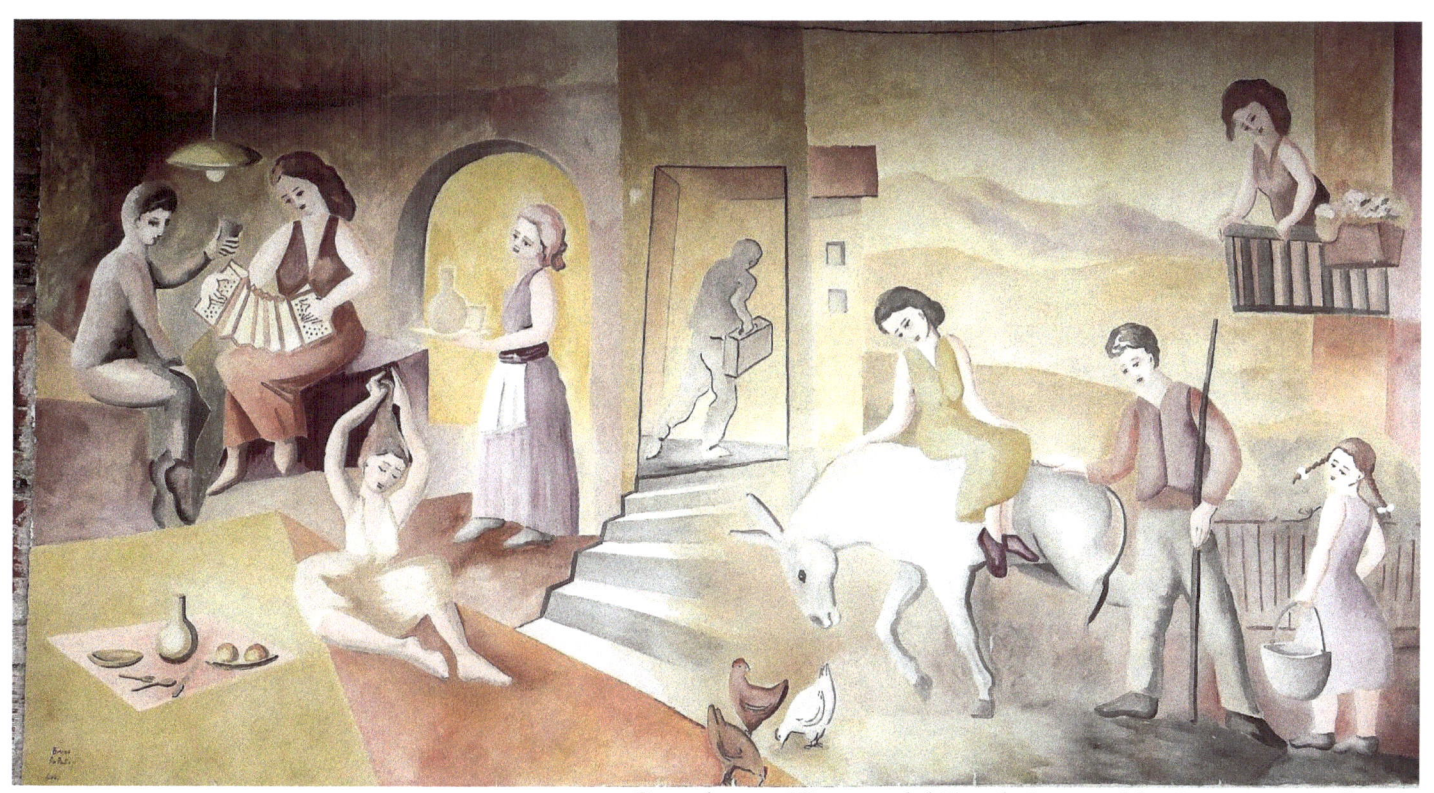

Costalunga (Cavaso del Tomba), mural by Bruno De Pellegrin

Fritoe, pancakes. In a large bowl melt the yeast crumbled in the lukewarm milk and add 50 gr. of flour, cover and let it rest covered until it has doubled in volume. Meanwhile soak the raisins in warm water (or rum) for half an hour. Take the leavened dough and add 200 gr. flour, egg, sugar, well-squeezed raisins, dried and floured, pine nuts, grated lemon rind, rum and a pinch of salt. Also add an apple into small pieces. Mix the ingredients well and leave to rise for an hour. Blend the dough well and throw it with spoonfuls (or teaspoons if you want fritters that are a bit smaller) in boiling oil a few at a time. Serve sprinkled with fine or icing sugar.

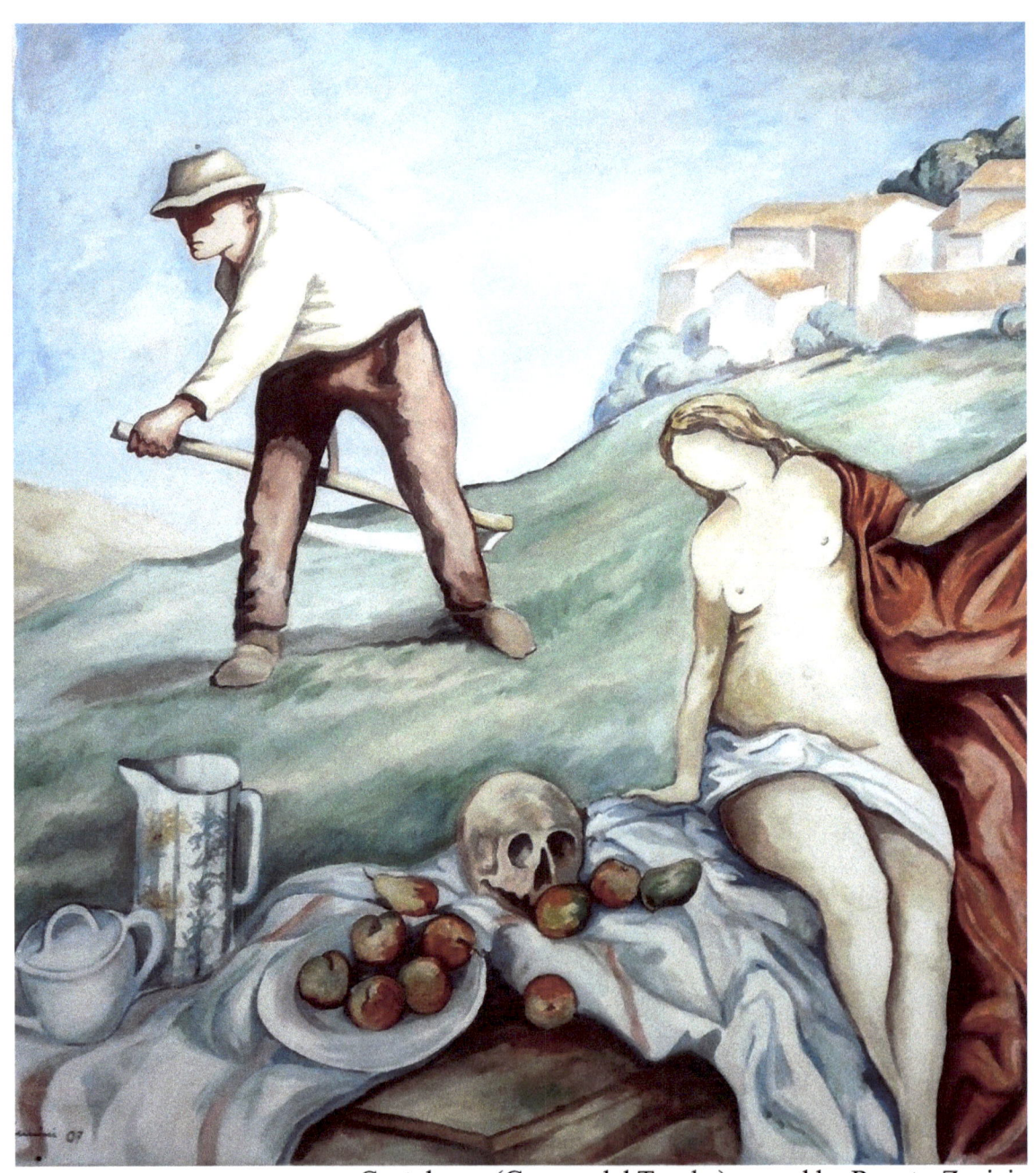

Costalunga (Cavaso del Tomba), mural by Renato Zanini

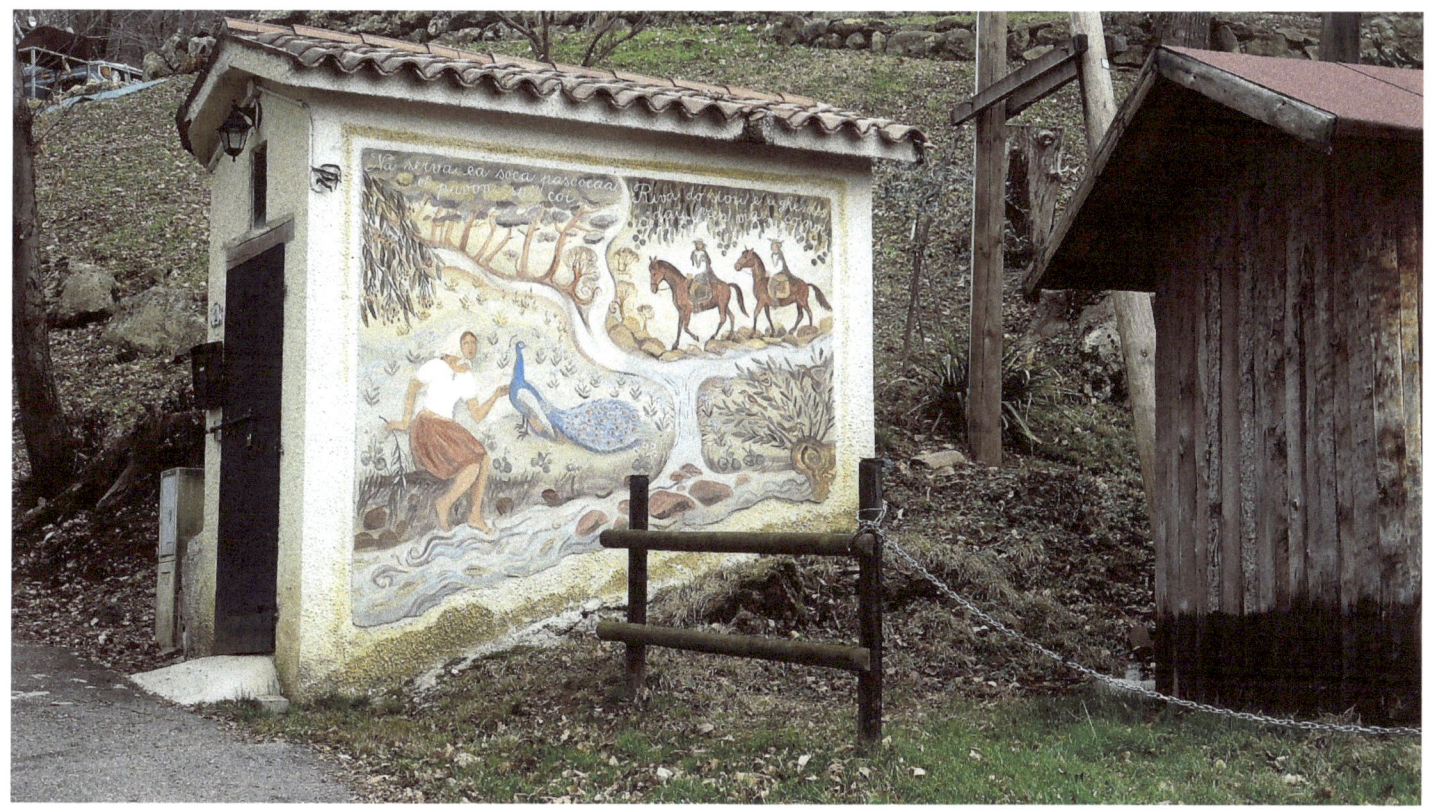

Costalunga (Cavaso del Tomba), mural

Frittelle con fiori di acacia, pancakes with acacia flowers. Collect the clusters of acacia (robinia) flowers, wash them carefully and dry them well. Mix three eggs with half a glass of milk, half a packet of yeast, three ounces of flour, a little olive oil and three drops of cedar or lemon flavor, until you get a creamy dough, but not too liquid. In a large saucepan, heat plenty of oil to fry and when it is hot, carefully dip the bunches dipped in the batter, being careful not to detach the flowers. Let them cook for a few minutes turning them from time to time to have a more uniform cooking. As they are ready, remove the fritters with a slotted spoon and let them dry on absorbent paper, then sprinkle with icing sugar and serve.

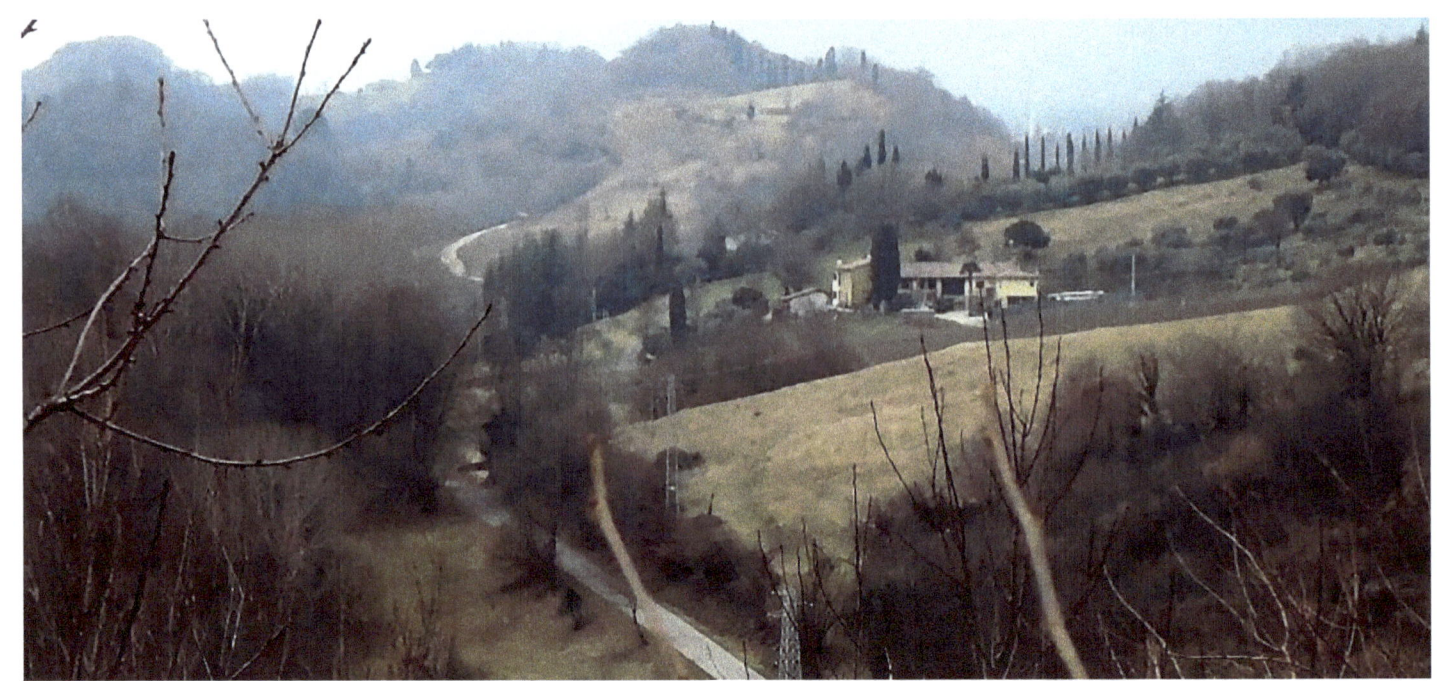
Costalunga (Cavaso del Tomba)

Frittelle con fiori di zucca, pancakes with pumpkin flowers. Put the flour, half a packet of yeast, a pinch of salt and the grated rind of a lemon in a bowl. Put the egg yolk in another bowl, add the sugar and whisk the cream ingredients with a whisk. Add the mixture to the flour and mix well. Add a tablespoon of grappa, one of olive oil and season with a pinch of cinnamon. Remove the pistil from the pumpkin flowers and clean them carefully with a damp cloth, being careful not to wet them. Stir in a glass of marsala and without stopping mixing dilute with a liter of milk poured flush. The batter should be homogeneous and fairly soft, making sure that no lumps form. In a pan heat plenty of oil, pass the flowers in the batter and dip them in the hot oil. Brown them well and remove with a shovel, putting them in a paper towel to lose the grease. Place them on a serving dish, sprinkle with icing sugar to taste and serve hot or lukewarm.

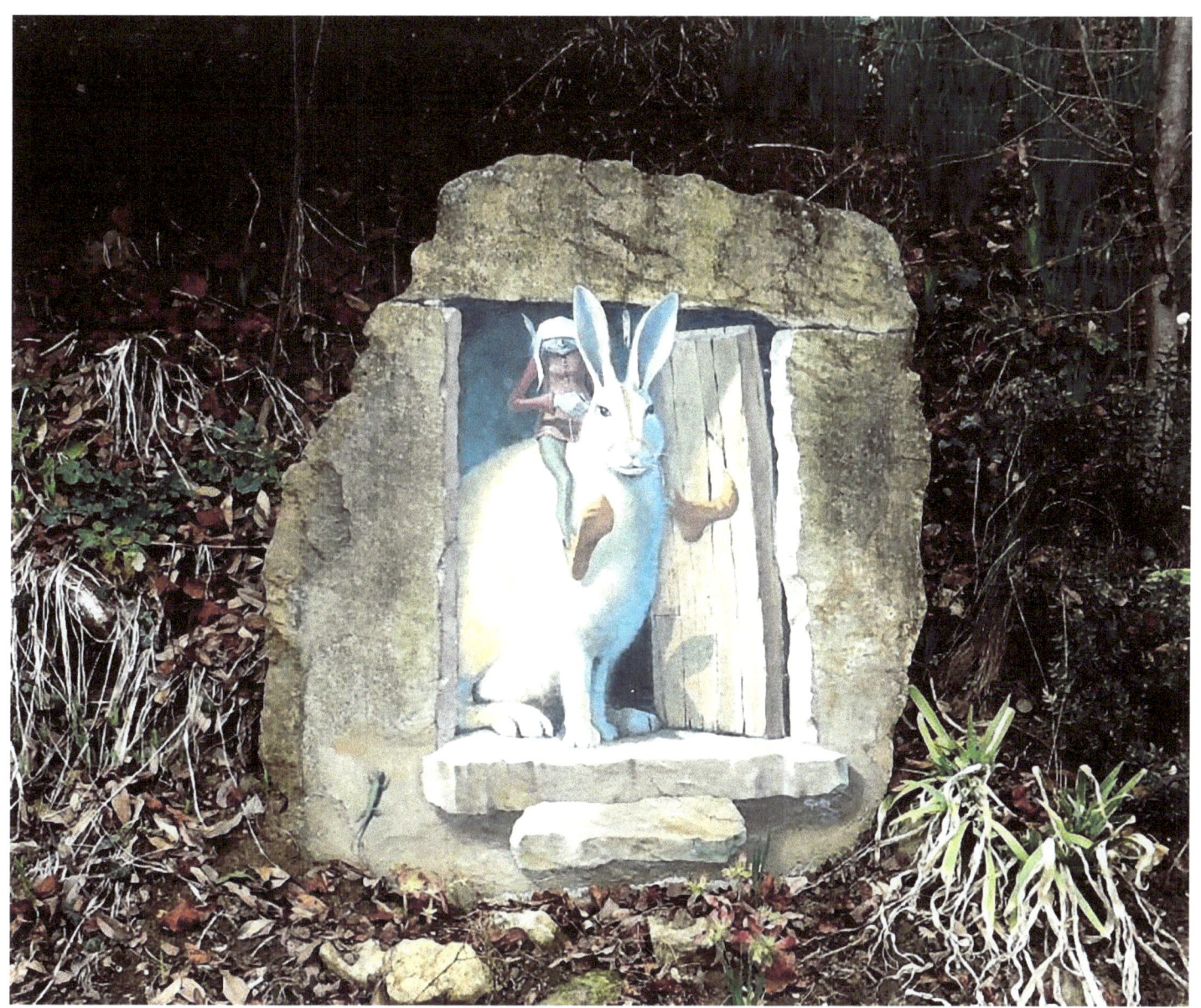
Costalunga (Cavaso del Tomba), mural

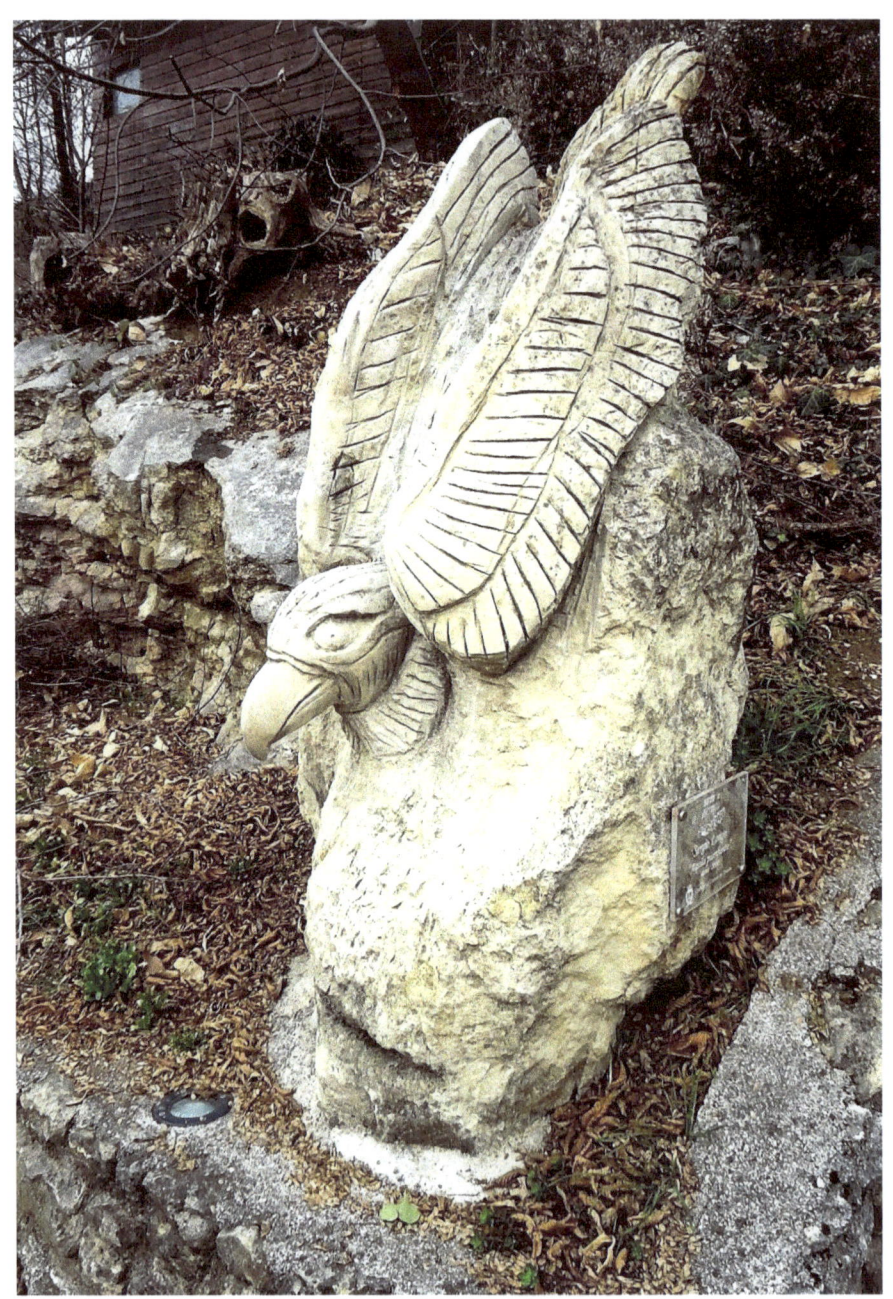

Costalunga (Cavaso del Tomba), artwork

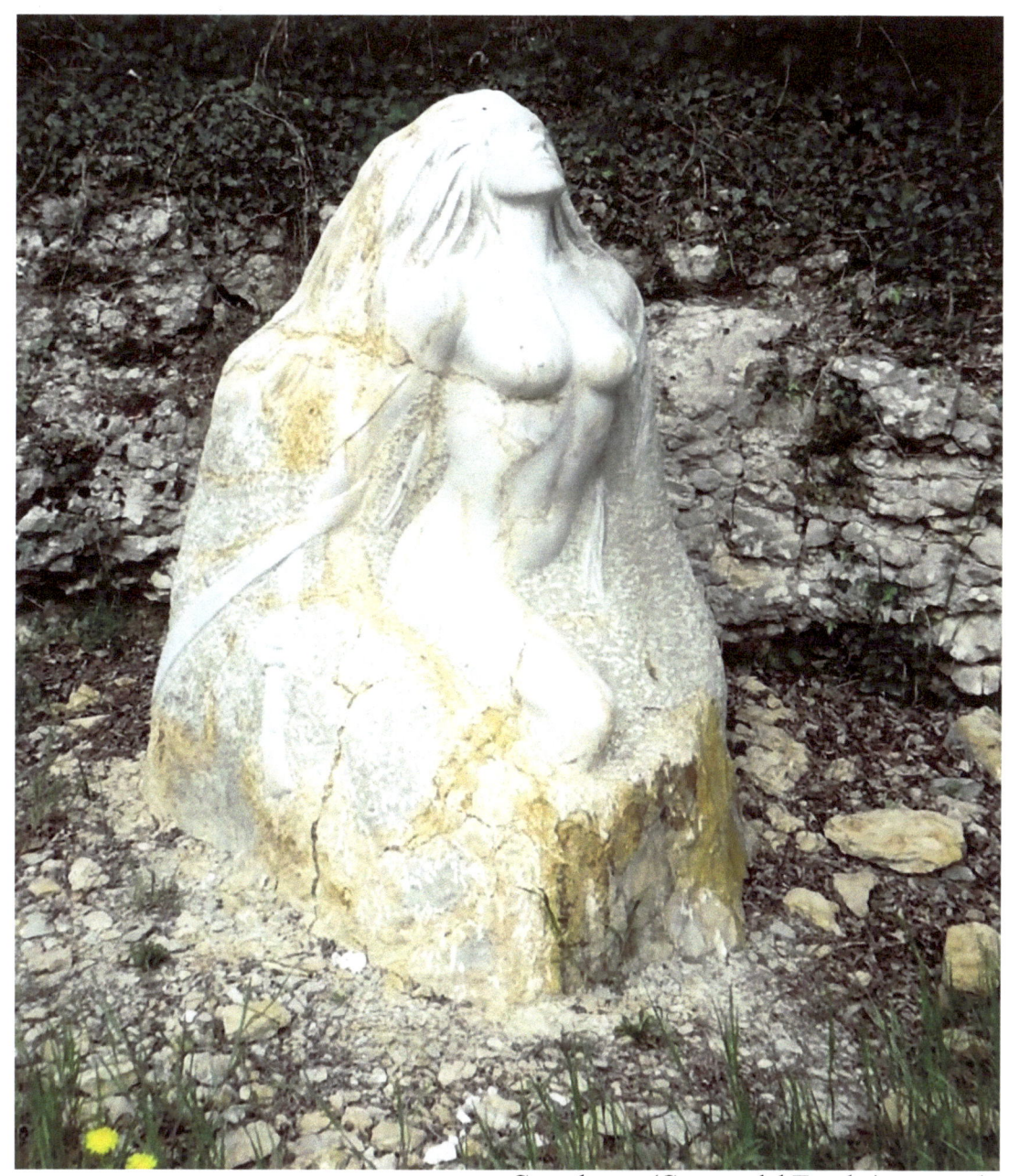
Costalunga (Cavaso del Tomba), artwork

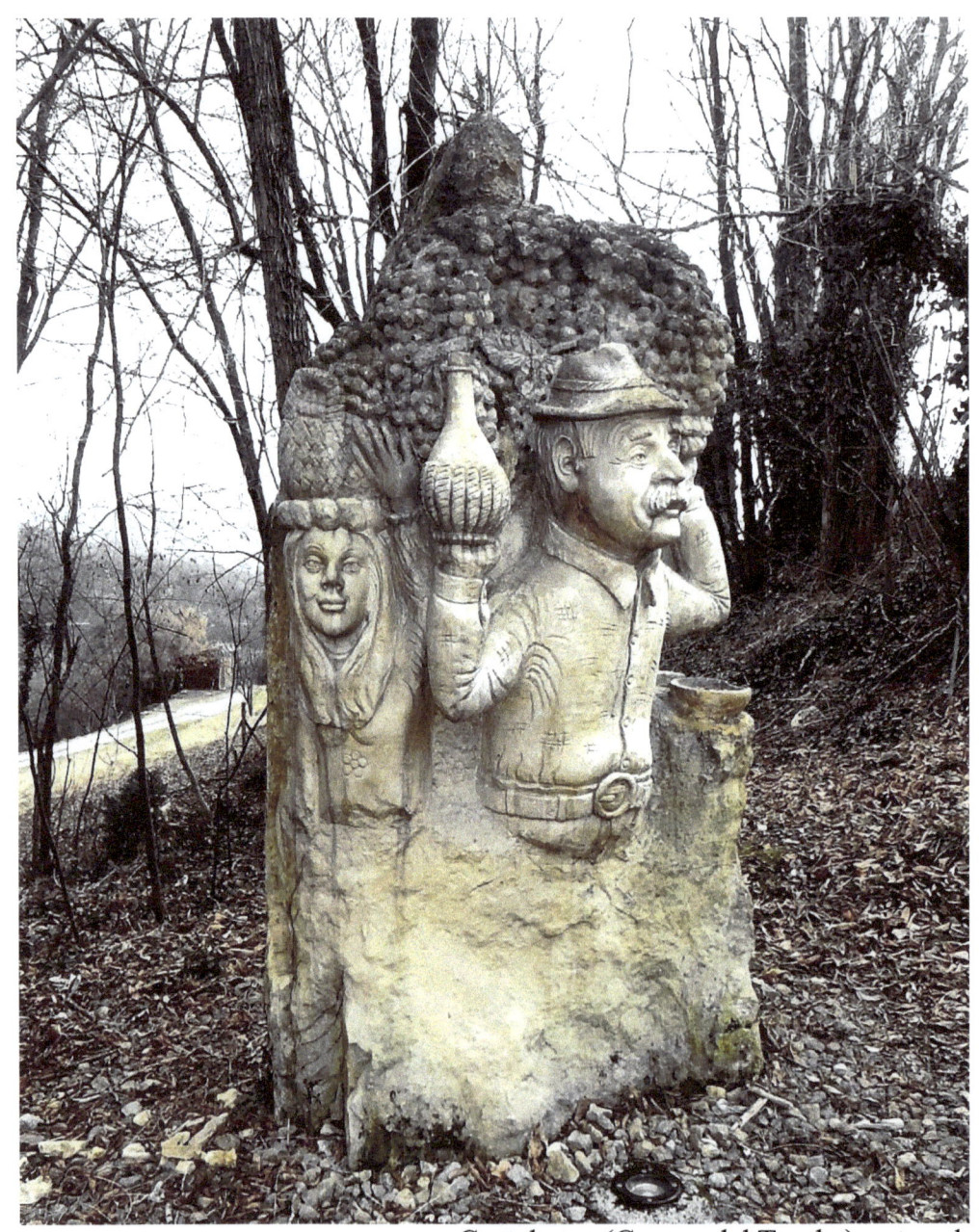
Costalunga (Cavaso del Tomba), artwork

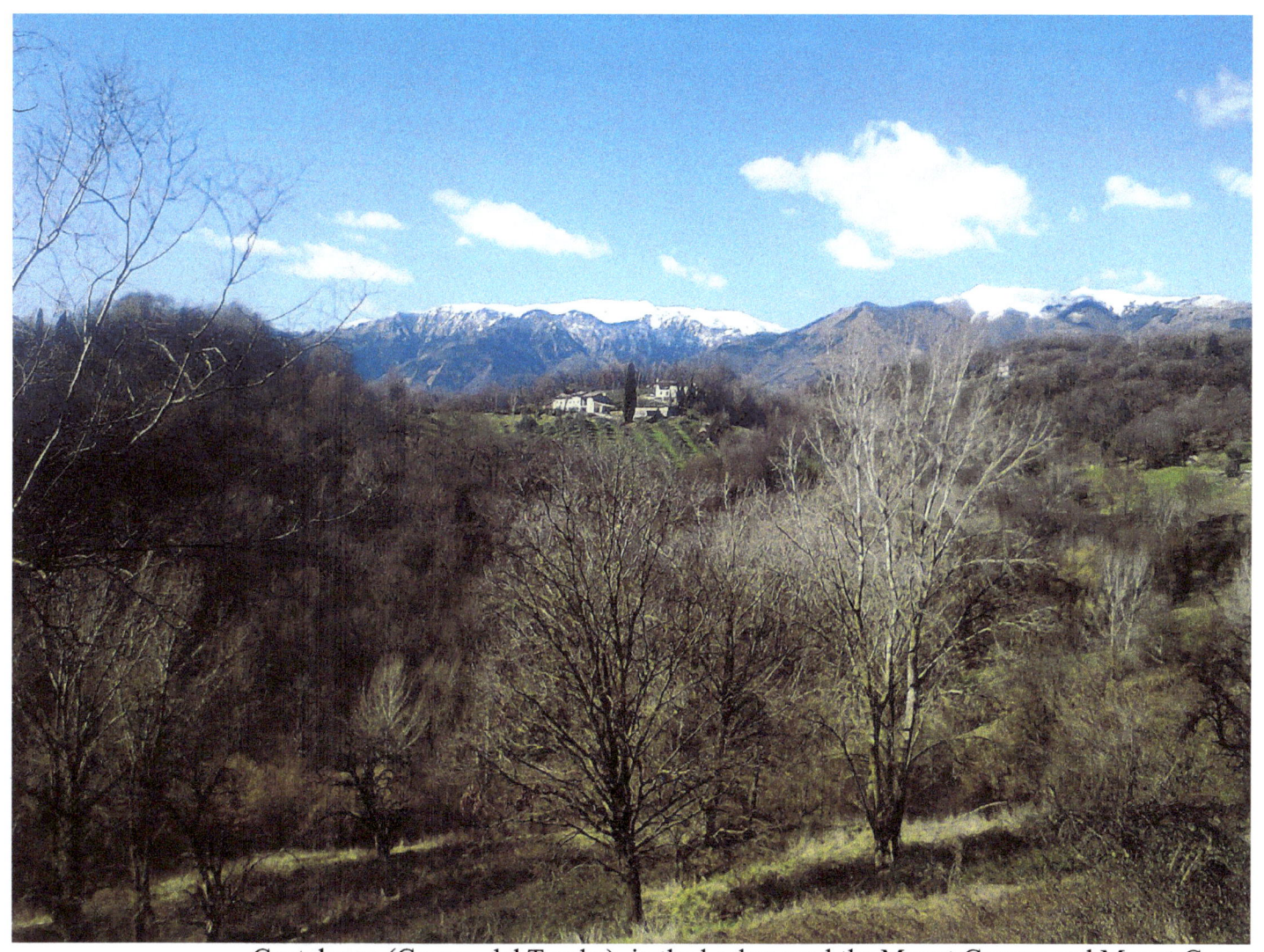
Costalunga (Cavaso del Tomba), in the background the Mount Grappa and Mount Cesen

Ghisola, the original typical dessert of Asolo created with the typical ingredients of the territory: Biancoperla corn flour and Monfumo apple jam. The recipe is reserved exclusively to professional pastry chefs and can be found in the pastry shops of Asolo and the surrounding area.

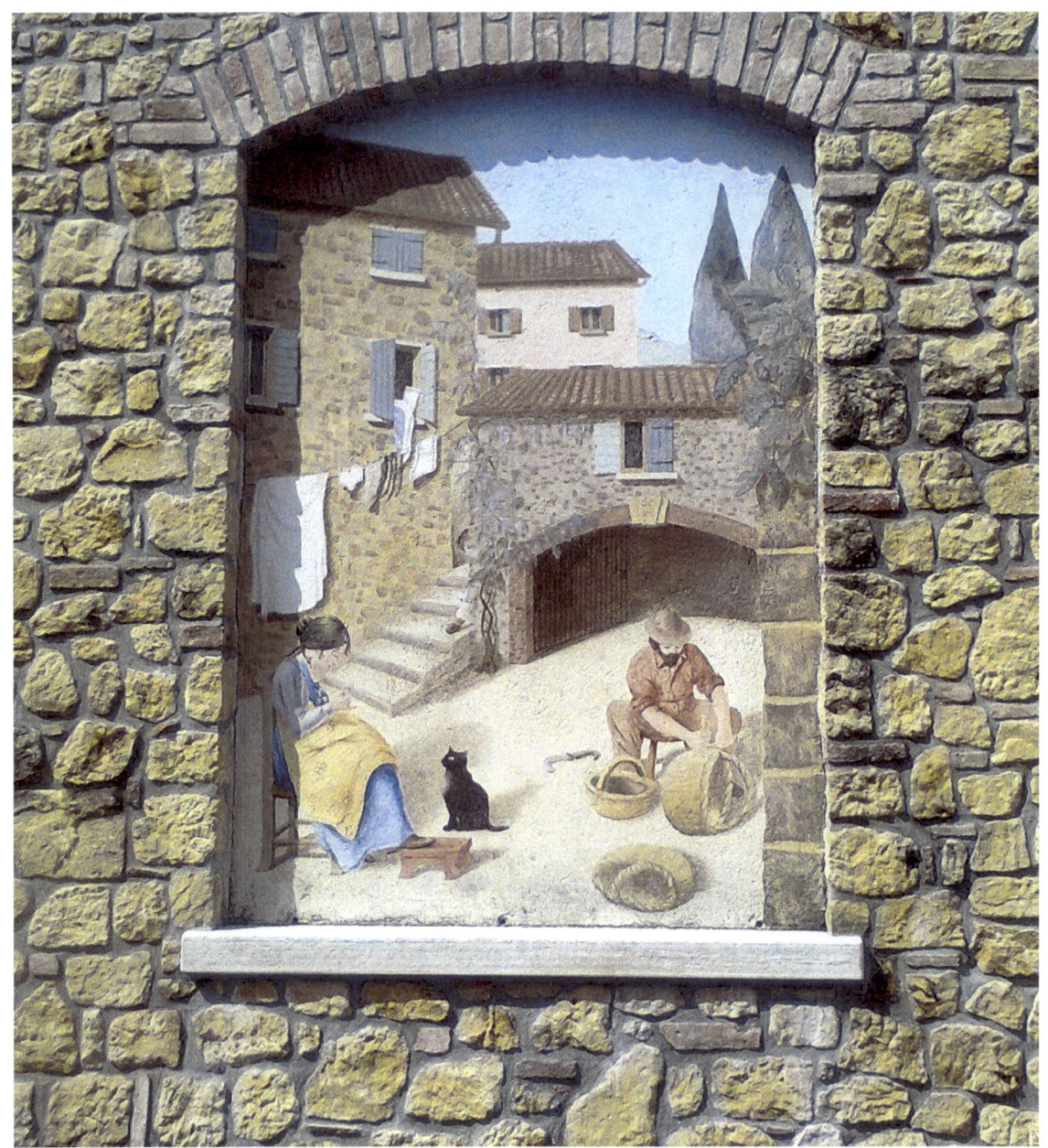

Bocca di Serra (Cavaso del Tomba), mural

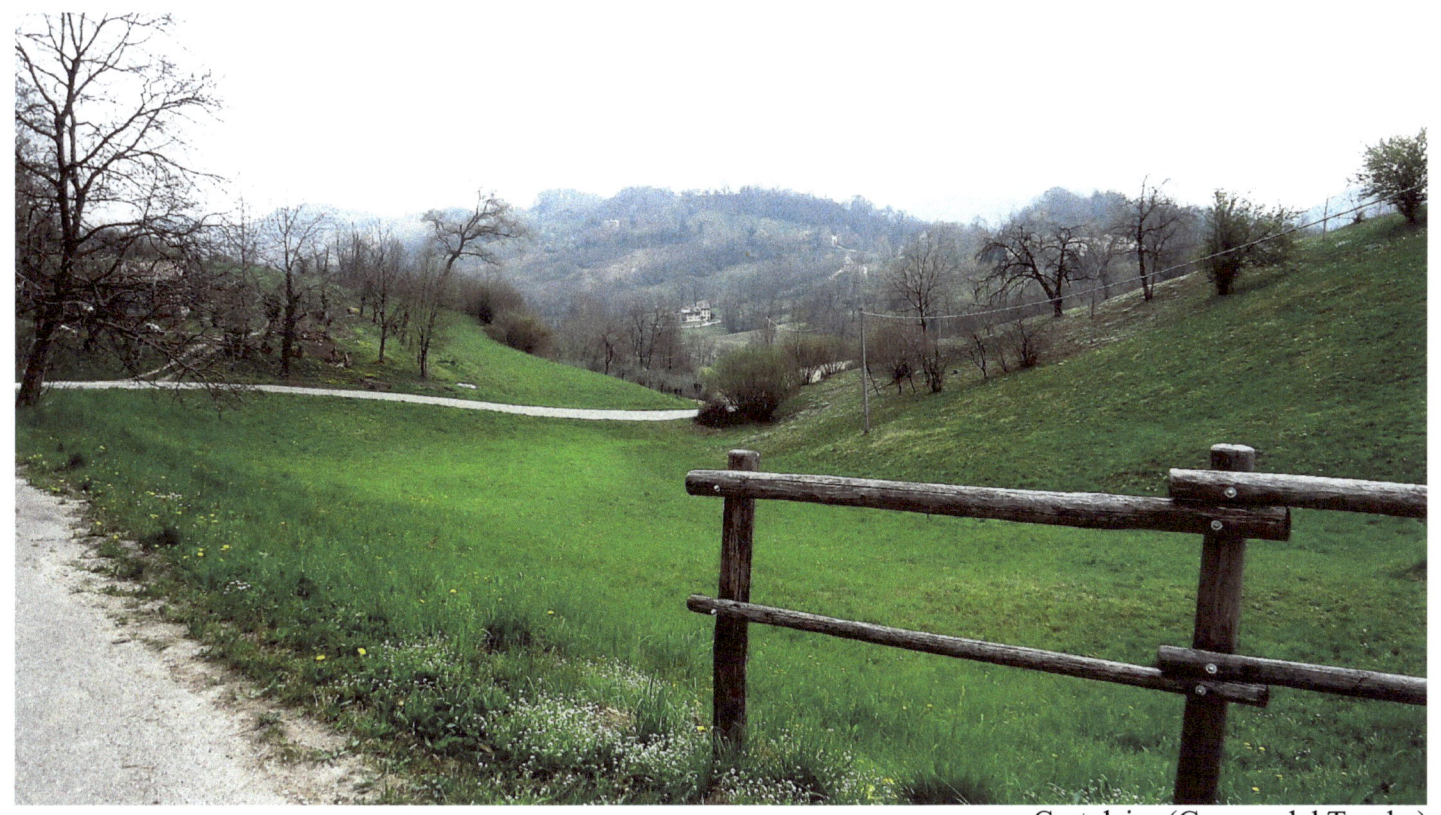
Castelcies (Cavaso del Tomba)

Pinsa. Cut the bread into small pieces, put it in a bowl, pour in the milk and leave it to soak for at least half an hour. Soften the sultanas in warm water and beat two eggs. Slowly add the flour, sugar and butter at room temperature, raisins, beaten eggs, a pinch of salt and mix everything together. Grease and sprinkle with breadcrumbs the high sides of cake pan, pour the mixture and sprinkle the fennel seeds on the surface. Bake at 180 ° in the oven for an hour. Let it cool in the mold, then take off it from the cake pan out and serve.

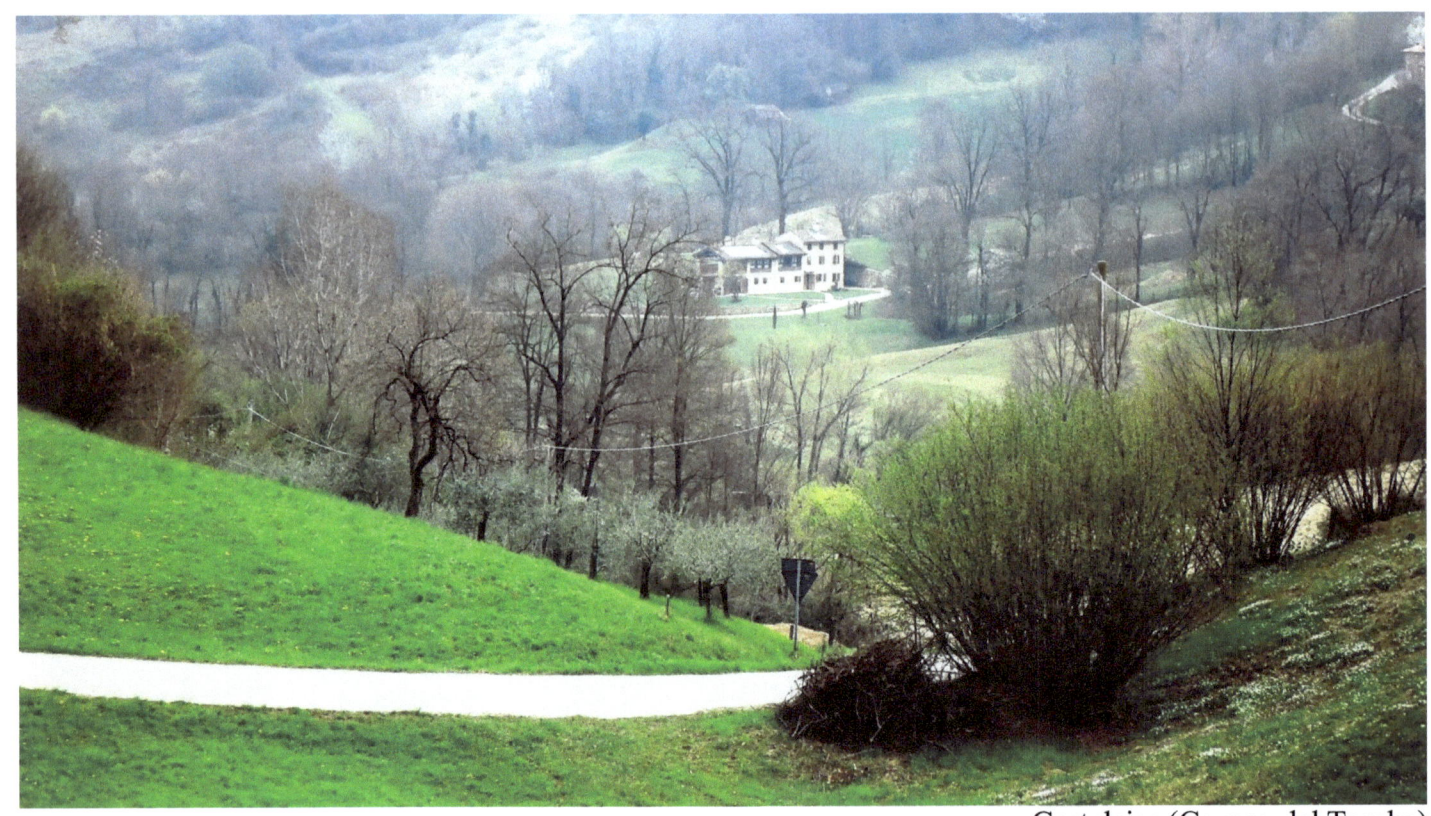
Castelcies (Cavaso del Tomba)

Tiramisu. Whip the egg yolks with the sugar until the mixture is light and whitish. Stir in the mascarpone gently until the mixture is smooth and thick. Soak the ladyfingers in cold and bitter coffee, place on the plate and cover them with a layer of cream, then more ladyfingers and cream until the dough is used up. The last layer should be of cream, because the bitter cocoa powder will be dusted on it. Let the dessert rest in the fridge and, if necessary, sprinkle with bitter cocoa again.

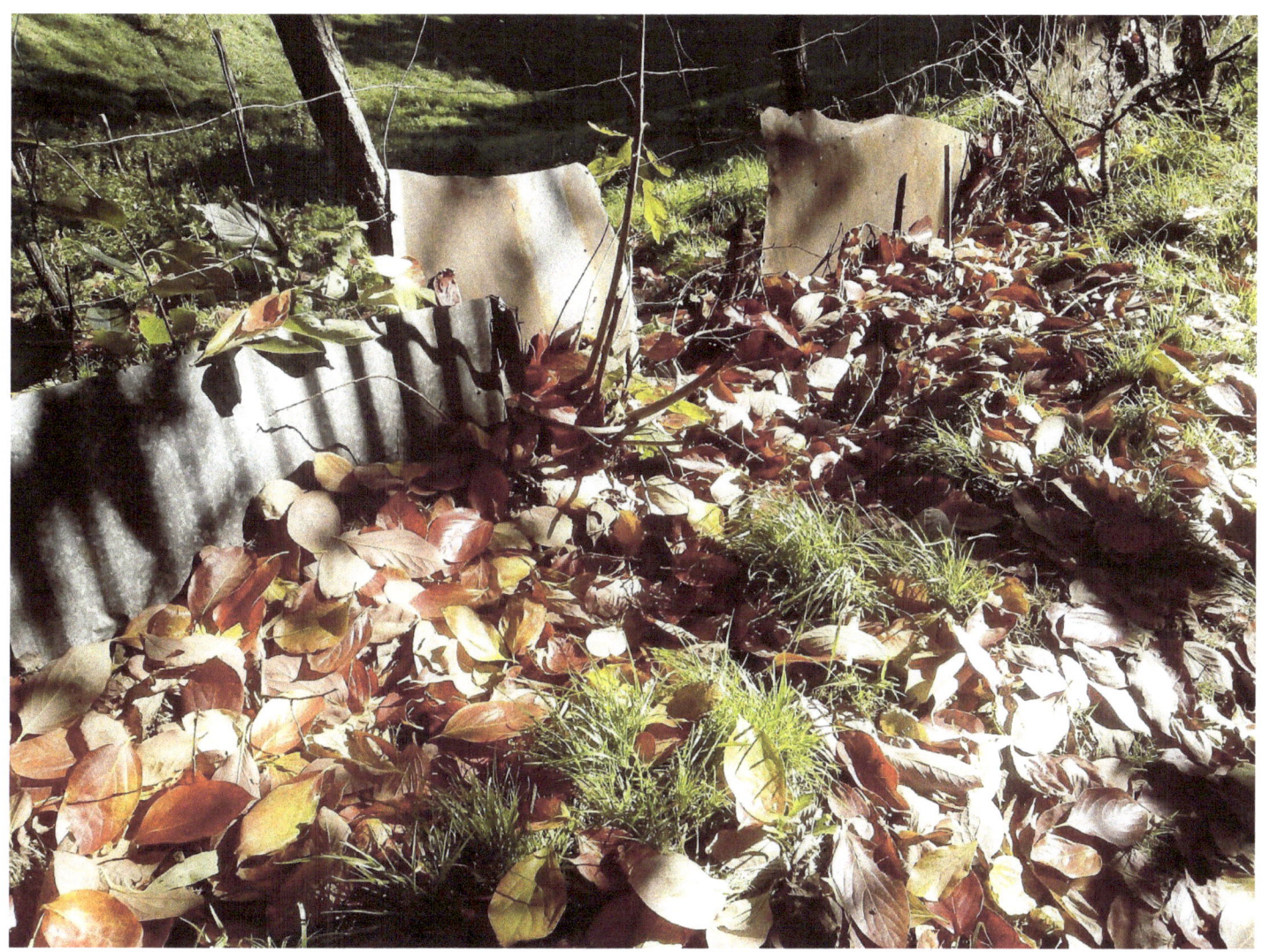
Onigo (Pederobba)

www.ingramcontent.com/pod-product-compliance
Lightning Source LLC
Chambersburg PA
CBHW051211220526
45473CB00003B/988